RELIGIOUS LIBERTY AND THE SECULAR STATE

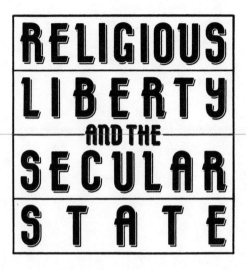

RELIGIOUS LIBERTY AND THE SECULAR STATE

THE CONSTITUTIONAL CONTEXT

JOHN M. SWOMLEY

PROMETHEUS BOOKS
700 East Amherst St., Buffalo, New York 14215

90 89 88 87   4 3 2 1

Library of Congress Card Catalog No. 86-25543
ISBN: 0-87975-398-6 (paper)
ISBN: 0-87975-373-0 (cloth)

Contents

Religious Liberty and the Secular State

A democratic society is a society whose major decisions are made either by the people or with the freely given consent of the governed. It is a society responsive to law that protects the rights of individuals and minorities to oppose the prevailing opinion and to express themselves in debate and action. Unless a free society is controlled by constitutional limitations placed upon government, there is nothing to restrain state absolutism.

Religious liberty is a crucial aspect of a free society. People must be free either to accept or to reject religion or particular expressions of religion. Otherwise, they have no freedom of choice to determine their beliefs and the institutions that embody their beliefs about the universe, human nature, peace, justice, and comparable matters.

Given the fact of strong religious conviction and competing religious groups, religious liberty can be guaranteed only in a secular state. A secular state is not hostile to religion. It can be defined as a state that is uncommitted to any religious institution or institutions or to religious beliefs and practices. Its basis for state authority is in civil and natural law, not in religious doctrine or in divine revelation. As the Supreme Court said in *Watson* v. *Jones* (1872): "The law knows no heresy, and is committed to the support of no dogma, the establishment of no sect."[1]

Philip Schaff, a distinguished American church historian in the nineteenth century, wrote that the U.S. Constitution "is neither hostile nor friendly to any religion; it is simply silent on the subject, as lying beyond the jurisdiction of the general government."[2]

The idea of a secular American state came from two sources. The first source was religious leaders who believed in the inalienable right of conscience and also in the principle of voluntarism in religion. They believed that genuine obedience to God must be uncoerced. Coercion cannot produce inward conviction. Separation of church and state was required to prevent church use of state machinery to coerce as well as to prevent state interference with religion.

The second source was John Locke, a philosopher whose writing influenced early political leaders. Locke said that everyone is born with natural rights to life, liberty, and property. He believed that the authority of the state is derived from the consent of the governed who create the state for their own convenience and for the public welfare. Since the state is a human invention and the state's laws are human laws, there is no basis either for the deification of the state or for anything other than a secular state.

A secular democratic state is compatible with all of the different religious views of the universe and with all religious organizations precisely because it supports no religious faith, no religious institution, and no dogma. It can therefore treat all equally. This is a very important attribute of the state because the long history of church-state relationships is one of state support of churches that claim to have the true faith. When there is no separation of church and state and no secular society, there is more likely to be religious toleration than religious liberty.

Toleration means putting up with or enduring someone or something with whom or with which you disagree. Sanford Cobb's description is helpful: "toleration assumes that all are not equal, that one form of religion has a better right, while for the sake of peace it consents that they who differ from it shall be allowed to worship as shall best please themselves. Toleration, then, is a gift from a superior to one who is supposed to occupy a lower station in the scale of rights."[3]

The idea that the United States is a Christian nation presumes tolerance of Jews and other non-Christians. The idea once held in the United States that we are a Protestant nation that permitted freedom of worship for Roman Catholics is also evidence of toleration. Tom Paine wrote: "Toleration is not the opposite of intolerance but the counterfeit of it. Both are despotisms: the one assumes to itself the right of withholding liberty of conscience, the other of granting it."[4] Toleration is a concession; religious liberty is a right.

Genuine religious liberty involves not only freedom of choice, but also the equality of all, so that in matters of faith, and membership or nonmembership in religious institutions, there are no special privileges and no second-class citizens. Every person and every religious or nonreligious group should be equal before the law. Those religious groups that proclaim one Creator of all humans and, therefore, the brotherhood and sisterhood of all believe, at least theoretically, in the equality of everyone before God. Probably most religious groups would also publicly acknowledge equality before the law. However, some would negate it by political action designed to secure special benefits for their own institutions.

Legal fictions have been created to give the appearance

of equality of treatment. An illustration is the promotion of legislation to secure tax deductions for tuition, transportation, and textbooks for public and nonpublic schools when only church or other private schools charge tuition and pass on transportation and textbook costs to parents. When a few denominations emphasize weekday parochial schools as a major mission of their church and expect tax deductions for tuition, transportation, and books to their schools, there is no equality with churches whose religious education takes place on Saturday, Sunday, or in summer camps. No deductions are permitted for tuition to colleges and universities where the children of all denominations and of none attend. Tax deductions for contributions to any nonprofit organization involve equality of treatment, as all churches, synagogues, and secular groups can use such benefits. The additional deduction granted to parents of parochial school children is unequal treatment.

Another legal fiction to justify aid to churches that operate weekday religious schools is the child benefit theory. With respect to bus transportation to parochial schools, the claim was made that if transportation were provided for children to attend public schools, it should be provided equally for those attending parochial schools because it is of benefit to children. However, transportation only to educational institutions benefits the school. With the advent of school buses, larger and better equipped schools could be built at greater distances from children than the traditional neighborhood school. The buses do not pick up school children because of hazardous intersections or bad weather, but because of distance from the school.

There is a difference between subsidizing transportation

for all children impartially and aiding pupils because they attend private religious schools. A genuine child benefit theory would not exclude children attending parochial schools if all children between 6 and 16 years of age were given half fare or full transportation every day for any purpose, including visits to parks, the zoo, or to sports, theatrical, educational, religious, and other events. The function of a secular state is impartial administration of justice, not rationalization of state aid to one or more powerful religious groups.

A secular democratic society would neither penalize nor reward anyone for his or her religious beliefs. The state has no responsibility to support or aid religion in any way. If the state supports one denomination, it compels those members of other religious institutions to support a religion with which they do not agree. If they are compelled through taxes to support their own church projects, it may be in a different amount than they would voluntarily have given. If a state aids a church that claims it cannot otherwise maintain its weekday schools or other church projects, the state may be taking sides with administrators of a church whose laity are not giving because of disapproval of church policy or failure to account publicly for its contributions and use of funds. In other words, state aid may be interference with the reformation of churches.

If the state tries to support all religions, it compels those who claim no religion to support what they do not believe—something that is not appropriate to the democratic process. Actually, it is impossible for the government to aid equally more than 300 religious organizations of varying sizes and differing projects. Therefore, aid to all religions is necessarily preferential aid to the most politically influential or to those with a larger number of church projects, such as hospitals, schools, and homes for children. Equality of all religious bodies before the law is possible only in a secular state. The religious liberty of all necessarily requires that no church, synagogue, denomination, or combination of religious organizations have the power to direct the government, its policies, or actions other than through the process of persuading public opinion on the issues or principles they advocate.

It is also essential that the government not institute its own religious activity either as a supplement or as an alternative to the religious expression of individuals or churches and synagogues. If government officials believe private religious expression is not adequate, or that the general public needs to be exposed to state-sponsored prayer services or religious gatherings under public auspices such as in public schools or in connection with public sports events, such state activity would violate religious liberty. The mere fact of prayer authorized by law is a civil matter and therefore a secular rather than religious expression.

The use by the state (and even by secular business corporations) of religious services and symbols secularizes and profanes them. The Bank of the Holy Spirit in Lisbon, Portugal, does not differ from other banks in interest rates charged to the poor or in its employment practices. When the government takes over a religious holiday or sponsors religious displays, it endorses the appearance of religiosity without the ethical and theological substance of the religion it endorses. In this way, because government is not a community of faith, it waters down and secularizes the otherwise sacred symbols. Government sponsorship of religious services, holy days, and religious symbols is thus an additional enemy of religious liberty and of religion itself.

In democracies or republics such as the United States, government rarely engages in such violations of religious liberty because it intends to secularize or to damage religion. It does so at the request of or as the result of pressure from organized religious groups. There are religious groups that believe that the state should not be an impartial administrator of justice or promoter of the general welfare but an agency to promote the true religion, which they believe is not only Christianity, but their particular expression of Christianity. Such groups retain legal and public relations staff for the purpose of gaining government aid or government expression of their position. Although such efforts over a period of decades are often counterproductive, religious bodies have a right to engage in such activity and to hold such beliefs, as do those who oppose their sectarian proposals or who oppose all religion.

Religious liberty cannot be founded on restriction of groups seeking dominance for their doctrines or organization, or on restriction of opponents of organized religion. Such restriction is the negation of liberty. The secular state, however, is constitutionally restricted and forbidden to legislate or otherwise involve itself in religious matters. That is the genius of the American doctrine of separation of church and state and of a secular constitution. Theocratic government, or something short of it in the way of government support or endorsement of religious doctrine or institutions, is a denial of religious liberty. Only when the state is secular can it be impartial and therefore guarantee equally the liberty of all religious organizations.

Some religious groups are critical of the idea of a secular state because they believe anything secular is an enemy of religion. This assumes that complete neutrality with respect to religion is hostility. This is not the American experience; religious influence in American society and church membership has grown substantially since the adoption of a secular constitution in 1787.

The following reasons summarize why churches should favor separation of church and state, which is the essence of a secular state:

(1) Separation prevents the government from determining church policy, whether directly or indirectly.

(2) Separation does not permit churches to seek special privileges from government that are denied to minority religious groups and to nonreligious citizens.

(3) Churches are healthier and stronger if they assume responsibility both for financing their own programs and for stimulating their members to accept that responsibility.

(4) By operating independently of government aid, the churches deny to government the imposition of compulsory tithes on all taxpayers, believers and nonbelievers alike. The churches thus avoid the resentment of those who do not want to be forced to contribute to churches to which they do not belong and of their own members who do not welcome being forced to contribute through government taxation.

(5) Since separation precludes financial support or special privilege from government, the churches are free to engage in prophetic criticism of the government and to work for social justice.

(6) The mission of the churches is compromised by

government aid to church schools and colleges that serve chiefly middle- and upper-class students or by government subsidy of church-sponsored homes for senior citizens of the same general economic status. Church empires are costly and require additional private funds from those who use the services, thus tending to exclude millions of poor people.

(7) Government sponsorship of religious activity, including prayer services, sacred symbols, religious festivals, and the like, tends to secularize the religious activity rather than make government more ethical or religious. Prayer at the dedication of a missile silo does not make the weapon less deadly; nor does prayer in the classroom increase respect for poor teaching or inspire good discipline.

(8) The churches' witness in other nations is greater if they are not identified with Western culture or with one or more specific governments. The Dutch Reformed Church in South Africa is identified with the white government and its apartheid policy. Judaism is identified with Israel and its Palestinian policy. The Roman Catholic church was the alter ego of the Franco dictatorship in fascist Spain and the Salazar dictatorship in Portugal. It is the official church in Ireland and identified with the Irish Republican Army in its war to absorb northern Ireland.

NOTES

1. 80 U.S. 679 (1872).
2. Philip Schaff, *A Journal of Church and State* (Waco, Texas: Baylor University, Spring 1965), vol. VII, no. 2, p. 175.
3. Sanford H. Cobb, *The Rise of Religious Liberty in America* (New York: Macmillan Co., 1902), p. 8.
4. Thomas Paine, *Rights of Man,* p. 58.

CHAPTER I

Separation of Church and State: The Original Intent

The constitutional doctrine of separation of church and state is a uniquely American contribution to government. It means that government has no authority to invade the field of religion, that government agencies may neither advance nor inhibit religion, and that government may not take account of a person's religion or lack of it in determining qualification for holding public office or for government employment. The only function of government with respect to religion is that of protecting the right of conscience, worship, autonomous control over doctrine, governance and resources of religious groups, and the private and public expression of religious conviction.

Separation of church and state does not mean separation of religion and politics. The religious or nonreligious person or group may freely engage in political speech and action that criticizes or supports government policies. Congress, however, has been able to limit lobbying by churches through the granting of tax exemption and tax deductibility of contributions to nonprofit agencies that use only a fraction of their resources to influence legislation.

The Constitution of the United States provides for a wholly secular government. Any action by the Congress, the Executive, or Judiciary that confers any benefit upon religious organizations or places any impediment in the way of religious expression that does not infringe the rights of others is a violation of the letter and spirit of the Constitution.

The Constitution, wrote the historian Charles A. Beard, "does not confer upon the Federal government any power whatever to deal with religion in any form or manner."[1] James Madison called it "a bill of powers." He said that "the powers are enumerated and it follows that all that are not granted by the Constitution are retained" by the people.[2]

The Constitution must be understood as a social contract between the people and the United States. The Tenth Amendment spells out the meaning of the social contract in these words: "The powers not delegated to the United States by the Constitution, nor prohibited by it to the states, are reserved to the states respectively or to the people."

The social contract idea came from the political philosophy of John Locke, who had been a strong influence on many leading Americans, including Thomas Jefferson and James Madison. Partly under John Locke's influence, Jefferson and Madison came to believe that a government that was formed as a social contract had no power given to it to act on religious matters. Locke, who had popularized the social contract theory of government, asserted in his first *Letter Concerning Toleration* that "the care of souls cannot belong to the civil magistrate because his power consists only in outward force; but true and saving religion consists in the inward persuasion of the mind. . . ."

Locke's statement in modern language is the idea that true religion is a matter of faith and that, if a church cannot persuade its members to accept its doctrine or contribute to its work, it is not the business of government to enforce the faith or pay its expenses. Governor Mario Cuomo of New York in 1984 defended his position of not seeking laws against abortion, following the assertion by Catholic bishops that Catholic politicians could not draw a line between their personal faith and public policy, when he said: "We seem to be in the position of asking government to make criminal what we believe to be sinful because we ourselves can't stop committing the sin."[3]

The secular nature of the Constitution is clearly evident in the only reference to religion in it prior to the adoption of the First Amendment. That reference is in Article VI, Section 3, which forbids religious tests for public office.

Although the Declaration of Independence, produced only eleven years earlier, contains various religious terms such as "Nature's God," the "Supreme Judge of the world," and "Divine Providence," the Constitution has no such reference. It refers incidentally to religion in that Sundays are not to be counted in the number of days within which the president may veto legislation.[4] This absence of religious references does not reflect any hostility to religion or even imply its unimportance. Rather, it is a recognition that religion would thrive better if left uninfluenced, unaided, and unimpeded by government.

Article VI, Section 3, which is the first specific statement of separation of church and state other than the secular nature of the Constitution itself, says:

> The Senators and Representatives before mentioned, and the members of the several State Legislatures, and all executive and judicial officers both of the United States and of the several States, shall be bound by oath or affirmation to sup-

port this Constitution; but no religious test shall ever be required as a qualification to any office or public trust under the United States.

This section is significant not only because it permitted any person without regard to religion to hold public office, but also because it provided for the use of "affirmation" as an alternative to a religious oath. An affirmation was understood as a solemn declaration by a person conscientiously opposed to taking an oath but which is parallel to the religious oath in value and penalty if violated.

The impact of this section of the Constitution has been of major significance to religious liberty. In itself it was an important impediment to the establishment or government support of any church. One reason for this is that the unchurched as well as adherents of churches dissenting to establishment were numerically larger than the combined memberships of all the churches that were formerly established during the colonial era or of those that could have had aspirations of such support at the time the Constitution was adopted.[5]

Anson Phelps Stokes, in his monumental work *Church and State in the United States,* wrote that "Congress as constituted with men and women from all the denominations could never unite in selecting any one body" as an established church. "This has been so evident from the time of the founding of the government that it is one reason why the First Amendment must be interpreted more broadly than merely as preventing the state establishment of religion which had already been made almost impossible."[6]

Stokes's statement is supported by comments made by contemporaries of the framing of the Constitution. Oliver

Ellsworth, a member of the Continental Congress from Connecticut, a delegate to the Constitutional Convention, and the third Chief Justice of the United States Supreme Court, noted in one of his writings that in European nations with established churches there were always religious tests for holding office.[7] Edmund Randolph, a delegate to the Constitutional Convention and the first Attorney General of the United States, referred to "no religious" tests for public office as meaning that those in office "are not bound to support one mode of worship or to adhere to one particular sect." Therefore, given the variety of religious organizations in the United States, "they will prevent the establishment of any one sect, in prejudice to the rest and forever oppose all attempts to infringe religious liberty."[8]

James Iredell, a Supreme Court Justice from 1790 to 1799, who served in the North Carolina Convention that ratified the Constitution, referred to the exclusion of a religious test for public office as one way to establish religious liberty. He said that Congress had no power to create "the establishment of any religion whatsoever; and I am astonished that any gentleman should conceive that they have. . . . If any future Congress should pass an act concerning the religion of the country, it would be an act which they are not authorized to pass, by the Constitution. . . ."[9]

Another North Carolinian, Richard Dobbs Spaight, who had been a delegate to the Constitutional Convention, said about religion, "No power is given to the general government to interfere with it at all. Any act of Congress on this subject would be a usurpation."[10]

Although the members of the Constitutional Convention and many other Americans believed that the new federal government had no power to legislate with respect to religion, there were many who feared the usurpation of power. They wanted to have a bill of rights that would effectively prevent the federal government from meddling with religion. Thomas Tredwell of New York opposed ratification of the Constitution, arguing that it needed a bill of rights. He said that he wished that "sufficient caution had been used to secure to us our religious liberties, and to have prevented the general government from tyrannizing over our consciences by a religious establishment—a tyranny of all others most dreadful and which will assuredly be exercised whenever it shall be thought necessary for the promotion and support of their political measures."[11]

Even in Virginia, James Madison and others who favored a federal union could not persuade the state convention to ratify the federal Constitution until it accepted a recommendation for a bill of rights. The opposition to ratification was led by Patrick Henry and George Mason. Mason had been a delegate to the Constitutional Convention in Philadelphia, but had refused to sign the Constitution because it did not have a bill of rights. He had been the principal author in 1776 of Virginia's Declaration of Rights. One of Virginia's proposed amendments to a federal bill of rights stated that "no particular religious sect or society ought to be favored or established by law, in preference to others."[12]

Although Virginia ratified the Constitution, Rhode Island and North Carolina did not do so until after Congress had adopted the Bill of Rights.

The first Congress produced the Bill of Rights, but without the unanimous enthusiasm of all its members. Some members of the Congress opposed the proposal for a bill of rights on the ground that it was unnecessary because the Constitution did not grant the government any power to deal with religion or other rights retained by the people. James Madison originally shared this view. He told the Virginia convention, June 12, 1788, prior to its ratification of the Constitution: "There is not a shadow of right in the general government to intermeddle with religion."[13] Madison, however, felt duty-bound to respect the Virginia convention's recommendation of a bill of rights. He also had come to believe that a bill of rights was needed to make doubly sure that Congress would not exercise powers not granted to it under the Constitution.

However, Madison was fearful that a bill of rights might be construed by future advocates of governmental power as implying that the government had implied powers that were not specifically denied to it.[14] Madison's fears have been realized, as we shall see in subsequent chapters.

NOTES

1. Charles A. Beard, *The Republic* (New York: Viking Press, 1944), p. 166.
2. *Annals of the Congress of the United States* (Washington: Gales and Seaton, 1834), vol. 1, p. 438.
3. *New York Times,* September 14, 1984.
4. Article I, Section 7.
5. William Warren Sweet, *Religion in Colonial America* (New York: Charles Scribners Sons, 1953), pp. 344-336.
6. Anson Phelps Stokes, *Church and State in the United States* (New York: Harper and Brothers, 1950), vol. 1, p. 527.
7. Paul L. Ford, ed., *Essays on the Constitution of the United States* (Brooklyn: The Historical Printing Club, 1892), p. 168.
8. Jonathon Elliot, ed., The Debates in the Several State Conven-

tions on the Adoption of the Federal Constitution in Five Volumes (Philadelphia: J. B. Lippincott and Company, 1941), vol. 3, p. 204.

9. Ibid., vol. 4, p. 194.

10. Ibid., p. 208.

11. Ibid., vol. 2, p. 399.

12. Ibid., vol. 3, p. 659.

13. Gaillard Hunt, ed., *Writings of James Madison* (New York: G. P. Putnam's Sons, 1900-1909), vol. 5, p. 176.

14. James Madison to Thomas Jefferson, October 17 and December 8, 1788, *The Papers of James Madison*, ed. Robert A. Rutland et al. (Charlottesville: University of Virginia Press, 1976), 11:295.

CHAPTER II

The Historical Context of the Establishment Clause

The Establishment Clause of the First Amendment, "Congress shall make no law respecting an establishment of religion," has become a source of controversy. Those who seek aid for parochial schools and other church projects have claimed that the Establishment Clause authorizes aid to churches on a nonpreferential basis. Some government leaders share this position. The most articulate representative of this position is Supreme Court Justice William H. Rehnquist.

The Supreme Court's Chief Justice, William H. Rehnquist, in his dissent in the Alabama prayer case, *Wallace* v. *Jaffee* (1985), not only attacked Jefferson's concept of a wall of separation between church and state, but also tried to reinterpret the meaning of the Establishment Clause to justify aid to religion. He said: "The framers intended the Establishment Clause to prohibit the designation of any church as a 'national' one." In addition, he wrote that the "Clause was also designed to stop the Federal Government from asserting a preference for one religious denomination or sect over others."[1] In other words, nonpreferential aid to religious denominations or religion in general is, in Rehnquist's terms, constitutional.

Rehnquist insisted that "the true meaning of the Establishment Clause can only be seen in its history."[2] The history begins with the historical context that created the need for the religion clauses of the First Amendment; it continued with the congressional decisions about the clause. Neither the historical context nor the congressional decisions support the Rehnquist position.

Rehnquist made a common mistake in assuming that the phrase "establishment of religion" referred to European history and the single national established church, such as the Roman Catholic church in Spain or the Anglican church in England. However, those who drafted and supported the First Amendment were not recent immigrants from Europe. Many of their ancestors had lived in America for generations, so that European establishment was not their only experience.

The constitutional historian, C. Herman Pritchett, has summarized the American experience as follows:

> The phrase "establishment of religion" must be given the meaning that it had in the United States in 1791, rather than its European connotation. In America there was no establishment of a single church, as in England. Four states had never adopted any establishment practices. Three had abolished their establishments during the Revolution. The remaining six states—Massachusetts, New Hampshire, Connecticut, Maryland, South Carolina and Georgia—changed to comprehensive or "multiple" establishments. That is, aid was provided to all churches in each state on a nonpreferential basis, except that the establishment was limited to churches of the Protestant religion in three states and to those of the Christian religion in the other three states. Since there were almost no Catholics in the first group of states, and very few Jews in any state, this meant that the multiple establishment practices included every religious group with enough members to form a church. It was this

nonpreferential assistance to organized churches that constituted "establishment of religion" in 1791 and it was this practice that the Amendment forbade Congress to adopt.[3]

A brief survey of colonies and states that had multiple establishments of religion would amplify the above statement and also provide a better understanding of the ferment against established churches that led to the First Amendment's clause: "Congress shall make no law respecting an establishment of religion. . . ."

MASSACHUSETTS

Massachusetts in 1780, more than ten years before the ratification of the First Amendment, adopted its own bill of rights authorizing the legislature to provide for "the support of public Protestant teachers of piety, religion and morality. . . . And every denomination of Christians . . . shall be equally under the protection of the law."[4] Even before this adoption of "multiple establishments," Massachusetts in 1727 had moved away from taxing everyone to support the Congregational church, so as to include the Episcopal church, and in 1728 extended this to Baptists and Quakers. The Quakers, or Society of Friends, opposed this in principle and were exempted from church taxation in 1731.[5]

In Boston, however, there was voluntary support of churches and church schools rather than religious taxation.[6] A minister of the established church, one of the prominent Congregational ministers, Rev. Andrew Eliot, wrote to Thomas Hollis in England: "I wish our fathers had contrived some other way for the maintenance of ministers than by a tax. Thank God, we have none in Boston. I do not like anything that looks like an establishment."[7] Other members of the established church also disapproved taxation for religious purposes. One of these, James Sullivan, who was later elected Governor of Massachusetts, wrote about such taxation: "This glaring piece of religious tyranny was founded upon one or the other of these suppositions: that the church members were more religious, had more understanding, or had a higher privilege than, or a preeminence over those who were not in full communion, or in other words, that their growth in grace or religious requirements, gave them the right of taking and disposing of the property of other people against their consent."[8]

The struggle for religious liberty in Massachusetts was the struggle against taxation for religious purposes. In that struggle there was civil disobedience; there were appeals to the Court and to the Crown in faraway England. Societies were organized to fight the tax. Even after some denominations had won the right to be taxed only for their own churches or meetings, they continued to resist the tax, even on the nonpreferential basis by which all organized religious groups received tax funds. Finally, the state senate, which had refused to end establishment, voted in 1831 to submit the issue to the people. The vote, which took place in 1833, was 32,234 for disestablishment to 3,273 for keeping the multiple establishments of religion. It was a 10 to 1 vote, and in 1834 the amendment was made effective by legislation.[9]

NEW YORK

The Dutch Reformed church was initially the established church in the New Netherland. It was tax-supported.[10] When the English took over the colony, the Duke of York, the future James II, decided on religious toleration, evidently because of the religious diversity of the people and to provide a haven for Roman Catholics. He subsequently joined the Roman Catholic church. The duke's laws, written by the first English governor, Richard Nicolls, provided for a multiple establishment, which meant that each town by majority vote of the voters could provide a town church and levy taxes for its support. The churches, however, had to be Protestant.[11]

Subsequently, a series of royal governors tried to establish the Anglican church. After 1689, elective assemblies became the center of resistance to established churches.[12] Governor Benjamin Fletcher tried again and again to get the New York Assembly to make the Anglican church the established church. The assembly refused on two occasions, but in 1693, after "considerable pressure had been applied" by the governor, the assembly passed a law mentioning only "good sufficient Protestant" ministers and made it applicable only to the city and county of New York and the counties of Richmond, Queens, and Westchester. In all, six parishes were created.[13] Fletcher, on his own, then granted a corporate charter in 1697 designating Trinity Church (Episcopal) as the legally established church of New York City.[14]

In 1777, a state convention abrogated all establishment laws aiding denominations or ministers.[15] In 1781, the New York legislature adopted a policy of reserving land for the support of the Gospel and schools in state tracts being opened for settlement in upstate New York. But "there was no serious consideration of direct subvention of specific sects, that is to say for establishments literally understood."[16]

NEW HAMPSHIRE

New Hampshire was governed by an act passed in 1693 by His Majesty's Council for the Province of New Hampshire entitled "Maintenance & Supply of the Ministers and Schools Within This Province." It placed upon each town meeting the responsibility for selecting and paying the clergy, but permitted people of other churches to be excused from taxation for "the support of the Ministry of the Towne" provided that they conscientiously oppose the tax "and constantly attend the public worship of God on the Lord's day according to their owne P'rswassion. . . ."[17]

By the eve of the American Revolution, New Hampshire had Quakers, Episcopalians, Presbyterians, and a few Baptists as well as the large Congregational establishment. "According to the law any church which could gain majority recognition at the polls could create an established church in that town. . . . Some communities had a dual establishment."[18]

Over a period of time there was civil disobedience. People refused to pay the church tax. There were political campaigns for toleration rather than the system of multiple establishments. This culminated in the Toleration Act of 1819, which incorporated the practice existing at the time the Bill of Rights was adopted. That act provided that towns that had an existing contract with a settled minister could continue to collect taxes to fulfill that contract, but no person not of that religious persuasion "shall be liable to taxation for the purpose of fulfilling any contract. . . ."[19] The act also permitted "each religious sect or denomination of Christians" to raise money by taxes for church purposes "provided that no person shall be compelled to join or support . . . any congregation, church or religious society. . . ."[20]

It is significant that New Hampshire, with its experience of controversy over and opposition to established churches, produced the clearest proposal for separation of church and state in the first Congress, which considered and adopted the First Amendment. Samuel Livermore, an Episcopalian rather than a Congregationalist, who was also Chief Justice of the state, served as chairperson of the committee on amendments of the state constitutional convention called to ratify the federal Constitution. That committee, with the approval of the convention, recommended the following language for the religion clauses of the Bill of Rights: "Congress shall make no laws touching religion or to infringe the rights of Conscience." When Congress was considering an amendment that read: "no national religion shall be established by law," Livermore proposed instead that "Congress shall make no laws touching religion. . . ." His proposal was adopted, changed slightly, and "formed the actual basis of the final action."[21]

GEORGIA

Georgia had been organized as a royal province under the direct control of the king in 1754. There was a royal governor and a house of assembly elected by the people who owned at least 50 acres of land. Members of the house had to own at least 500 acres. The council appointed by the king was both a cabinet to the governor, an upper house of the assembly, and, with the governor, a court of appeals. The Act of 1758 established the Church of England. It was adopted after having been previously defeated in the upper house of the assembly. However, there were rarely more than two Anglican ministers in the colony at one time.[22]

The government of Georgia financed the Church of England, paying the ministers a small salary and building and repairing churches. Most of the tax came from liquor consumption and from property owners. When the American Revolution began, there were only two well-organized parish churches, one in Augusta and the other in Savannah. The establishment was therefore not burdensome enough to provoke a great protest by dissenters.[23] However, as settlers poured in from other colonies following the French-Indian War and from Europe, there were Baptists, Congregationalists, Presbyterians, and other dissenters who opposed the establishment law. By 1773, more than one-third of the assembly members were dissenters.[24] The decline of Anglicanism was also accelerated by the close connection between the church and the Tory cause.[25]

The first state constitution was completed in 1777. Free exercise of religion was granted. No one was to be forced to support any religious teacher other than those of one's own profession. In 1785, such a law taxing people to support their own religion was passed.[26] This meant that a number of churches were established by law for tax support.

The Constitution of 1789 no longer required legislators to be Protestant, but it did not forbid taxation for religion. Thus, Georgia had a number of establishments of religion at the time Congress adopted the First Amendment. The Constitution, however, did provide that no one shall "be obliged to pay tithes, taxes, or any other rate" for religious purposes "contrary to what he believes to be right, or hath voluntarily engaged to do."[27] This provision in the Constitution invalidated a law that provided not only for a property tax, but for a return from state funds to the county for the support of religion. All sects and denominations of the Christian religion were guaranteed "free and equal liberty and Toleration in the exercise of their Religion."[28]

MARYLAND

The founder of Maryland, Cecil Calvert, took a liberal position of nondiscrimination with respect to "any person professing to believe in Jesus Christ." In 1649, the colonial assembly adopted what is known as the Toleration Act, which provided toleration for all "professing to believe in Jesus Christ" who did not deny the Trinity or the divinity of Jesus. Those who did deny these doctrines were to "be punished with death and confiscation . . . of all his or her lands. . . ."[29] During Cecil Calvert's control, which ended following the English Revolution of 1688, he provided for voluntary support of churches. When Calvert was in England his enemies launched a revolution to discredit him and religious toleration. False stories of hardships suffered by Protestants were circulated under the leadership of a man named John Coode with the intent of establishing the Anglican church. Petitions were sent to King William and Queen Mary and were answered by supporters of Calvert. As a result of the turmoil, the king voided the charter, removed Calvert, and set up a royal province.[30]

The king sent Sir Lionel Copley to the colony as governor. Upon his arrival, he summoned an assembly, which adopted "An Act for the service of Almighty God and the Establishment of the Protestant Religion within this province." This act established the Church of England as the state-church of Maryland and set a tax of forty pounds of tobacco for "each taxable Person" to pay for the support of the clergy. A series of oppressive acts were taken against Roman Catholics and Quakers, who protested to London without avail.[31] However, the king rejected a law passed in 1700 that required "That the Book of Common Prayer and the administration of the Sacraments, with the rites and services of the Church, according to the use of the Church of England, the Psalter and Psalms of David, and morning and evening prayer, therein contained, be solemnly read by all and every minister in every Church, or other place of public worship, within this province." Since this was contrary to the Toleration Acts of England, another bill was adopted that extended toleration to Protestant dissenters and Quakers.[32] Catholics, however, were deprived of their civil rights and no priest was permitted to hold a service except within the limits of a "private family of the Romish communion." Fortunately, the laws were almost never enforced and before long "Roman Catholics were able unchallenged to assume their rights. . . ."[33]

In 1776, the Declaration of Rights of the Maryland Constitution was adopted with the statement that the government could not compel persons "to frequent or maintain . . . any particular place of worship or any particular ministry."

This marked the end of the Anglican establishment. However, the same declaration authorized the legislature to replace a single establishment with multiple establishments by levying "a general and equal tax for the support of the Christian religion, leaving to each individual the power of appointing the payment over of the money collected from him" to the church or minister of his choice.[34] When the state assembly met to implement this provision, the bill to implement was defeated. However, neither this provision of the declaration was repealed nor was separation of church and state written into law.[35]

CONNECTICUT

Connecticut had an established church virtually from the time the colony was established. It was the Congregational church, but at times during its colonial history Presbyterians were accepted as a branch of the established church. Strict enforcement of the establishment led to beatings of Quakers and Baptists. As a result of various appeals to England by Quakers and Episcopalians, some fear developed that the English Crown might have doubts about Connecticut's charter. The Episcopalians subsequently were able to persuade the General Court of Connecticut in 1727 to pass an act "providing how taxes levied upon members of the Church of England for the support of the Gospel should be disposed of," and exempting Episcopalians from paying any taxes "for the building of meeting houses for the present established churches of this government."[36]

This law with respect to Episcopalians was the beginning

of a multiple establishment since the taxes from Episcopalians were to be delivered to the "minister of ye Church of England living near unto such persons. . . ."[37] Two years later, Quakers and Baptists were granted exemption by the Connecticut court from paying taxes for the established church and taxes for their own meeting houses provided they could show a certificate that they regularly attended services.[38]

As a result of the writings and influence of Isaac Backus, the father of American Baptists, and the work of others, a mood of liberty of conscience began to develop and even reach into the establishment.[39] Many churches and societies were exempted from taxes at different times. An important "Act for Securing the Rights of Conscience" was adopted in 1784. This provided that Christians of every denomination who dissented from the established church and attended worship elsewhere should not be taxed for the support of other churches, and that Protestant dissenters should have the same right to tax money for their churches. However, those who did not belong to any religious society would continue to be taxed for the support of the state-church.[40]

The effect of this law was to extend most of the privileges of the established church to other Protestant denominations without eliminating the state-church. As a result, Connecticut, at the time the Bill of Rights was considered in Congress, had had a number of years of experience with multiple establishments. It was not until 1818 that Connecticut framed a new constitution "which destroyed all religious establishment." However, it dealt only with Christians, and a subsequent legislature construed it as applying also to Jews.[41]

SOUTH CAROLINA

A charter granted by Charles II of England and another granted in 1665 established the Church of England, but conceded a modified liberty to dissenters. Later members of the Church of England adopted harsh laws (1704) establishing the church and disenfranchising nonconformists. Since the majority of the people were nonconformists, many protests were sent to England. The result was the voiding of the laws in 1706 by the Queen in Council. Since South Carolina functioned as a part of The Carolinas, it did not become a separate province until 1729. The Church of England remained established.[42]

The constitution of 1778 declared the "Christian Protestant religion . . . to be the established religion of this state. All denominations of protestants in this State . . . shall enjoy equal religious and civil privileges."[43] This meant that the Anglican church was not disestablished, but that other churches were also established. However, this system of multiple establishments was voided by the constitution of 1790, which ended the Protestant establishment, enfranchised Roman Catholics, eliminated all provisions with respect to churches, and provided for religious freedom, "without distinction or preference," though it still excluded clergy from public office.[44]

It is not necessary to survey the states that never had an establishment of religion or those that abolished their establishments during the revolution. It is, however, essential to note that the question of establishment considered in the drafting of the First Amendment was an American and not a

European one. The overwhelming majority of the states in America that ever had established churches had multiple establishments and, hence, nonpreferential aid to churches.

In contemporary America the only church that has steadily sought substantial aid for its institutions is the Roman Catholic church. It is the bishops rather than the laity who make such decisions through the U.S. Catholic Conference (USCC). The USCC filed an *amicus* brief in the *Mueller* v. *Allen* case[45] in 1983 in an effort to reverse "no aid to religion" decisions of the U.S. Supreme Court. That brief indicated that the Supreme Court, beginning with the *Everson* decision[46] in 1947, relied too heavily on "Virginia disestablishment history" and that "the meaning of the religion clauses cannot be derived solely from the experience of any one colonial group or locale. . . ." It proposed instead "a sharp focus on the great diversity of religious practice among the states." However, that brief's discussion of diversity focused on matters of ecclesiastical detail, such as "assent to the doctrine of the Trinity" and the exclusion of "ministers from civil office."

The USCC brief said that "the great number of people who ratified the First Amendment in the states did not share a church-state tradition in common with Virginia or each other." That brief is mistaken. The common church-state tradition can be summarized as follows:

(1) Nine of the original thirteen states had a colonial practice of established churches financed by public tax funds.

(2) The revolution against establishment in all nine colonies was begun and continued by protest against tax support of religion.

(3) In single establishment colonies, an effort was made

to make public support of the established church tolerable by including other denominations in the establishment through the device of multiple establishments.

(4) Six of the states at the time of the Constitutional Convention had nonpreferential aid to religion in the form of multiple establishments.

(5) Prior to the ratification of the First Amendment, four states—North Carolina in 1776, New York in 1777, Virginia in 1779, and South Carolina in 1790—ended their establishments of religion, making a total of eight out of the thirteen that had no taxation for religious purposes. Maryland, which in 1776 adopted a constitutional provision for multiple establishments but never implemented it, would bring the total to nine states that were not providing public funds for religious purposes.

(6) At the time the First Amendment was adopted, the major uniform establishment practice remaining in the states was that of nonpreferential aid to churches.

The above summary reveals a common church-state tradition for most of the thirteen states, although they vary on details of doctrinal emphasis. It also shows that Virginia history is not unique, because it was one of nine colonies with established churches, one of nine where there was a significant protest against taxation for religious purposes, and one of four that disestablished before the First Amendment was ratified. However, it was unique in the caliber of religious liberty leadership of persons like Thomas Jefferson, James Madison, and George Mason, and in the quality of their statements for religious liberty. The lasting significance of Madison's *Remonstrance* and Jefferson's *Bill for Establishing Religious Freedom,* and of Jefferson's and Madison's national leadership for religious liberty or separation of church and state, are beyond dispute.

NOTES

1. *New York Times,* June 5, 1985.
2. Ibid.
3. C. Herman Pritchett, *The American Constitution,* 3rd ed. (New York: McGraw Hill, 1977), p. 401.
4. Henry S. Commager, ed., *Documents of American History* (New York: Appleton-Century-Crofts, 1949), p. 108.
5. Sanford H. Cobb, *The Rise of Religious Liberty in America* (New York: Macmillan Co., 1902), pp. 234-235.
6. Jacob C. Meyer, *Church and State in Massachusetts From 1740 to 1833* (Cleveland: Western Reserve University Press, 1930), p. 27.
7. Ibid., pp. 62-63.
8. Ibid., pp. 118-119.
9. Ibid., pp. 219-220.
10. John Webb Pratt, *Religion, Politics, and Diversity: The Church-State Theme in New York History* (Ithaca: Cornell University Press, 1967), pp. 8-9.
11. Ibid., pp. 29-30.
12. Ibid., pp. 37-38.
13. Ibid., pp. 40-41.
14. Ibid., p. 44.
15. Cobb, p. 502; Pratt, pp. 88-89.
16. Pratt, pp. 114-115.
17. Charles B. Kinney, *Church and State: The Struggle for Separation in New Hampshire, 1630-1900* (New York: Teachers College, Columbia University, 1955), pp. 36-37.
18. Ibid., pp. 78-79.
19. Ibid., p. 107.
20. Ibid., p. 108.
21. Anson Phelps Stokes, *Church and State in the United States* (New York: Harper and Brothers, 1950), vol. 1, pp. 315-317.
22. Reba Carolyn Strickland, *Religion and the State in Georgia in the Eighteenth Century* (New York: AMS Press, 1967), pp. 102, 103, 108.

23. Ibid., p. 113.
24. Ibid., p. 122.
25. Ibid., p. 162.
26. Ibid., pp. 163-164.
27. Ibid., pp. 164-165.
28. Ibid., p. 166.
29. Stokes, vol. 1, pp. 189-191.
30. Cobb, pp. 381-385.
31. Ibid., pp. 386-388.
32. Ibid., pp. 388-389.
33. Cobb, pp. 397-398.
34. John C. Rainbolt, "The Struggle to Define 'Religious Liberty' in Maryland, 1775-1785," *Journal of Church and State,* vol. 17 (Autumn 1975), p. 447.
35. Ibid., pp. 449-450.
36. M. Louise Greene, *The Development of Religious Liberty in Connecticut* (Freeport, N.Y.: Books for Libraries Press, 1970), p. 200.
37. Ibid., p. 201.
38. Ibid., pp. 215-217.
39. Ibid., pp. 329-333.
40. Cobb, p. 501.
41. Ibid., p. 513.
42. Ibid., pp. 115, 116, 125, 128.
43. Ibid., p. 505.
44. Ibid., p. 517.
45. 103 S. Ct. 3062.
46. *Everson* v. *Board of Education,* 330 U.S. 1 (1947).

CHAPTER III

The First Amendment: Its Origin and Meaning

When the first Congress convened, neither religion nor the Bill of Rights was uppermost in the minds of its members. It was James Madison who proposed and urged the Congress to adopt a bill of rights. Many of the members of Congress believed that it was unnecessary to have an amendment on the subject of religious liberty, because the Constitution did not grant any power to the federal government to deal with religion. One of those who articulated this position was Roger Sherman of Connecticut who, in the House debate, "thought the Amendment altogether unnecessary inasmuch as Congress had no authority whatever delegated to them by the Constitution to make religious establishments. . . ."[1]

Madison had originally shared this view, but had changed his position as a result of the debates in various state conventions over ratification of the Constitution. There were six states that either accompanied their ratification with specific recommendations for amendments in the nature of a bill of rights, or had not ratified the Constitution because it did not have a bill of rights. North Carolina and Rhode Island did not ratify until after Congress had adopted the Bill of Rights.

In Madison's own state of Virginia there was strong resistance to ratification because of the failure to include in the Constitution a guarantee of religious liberty. Madison, however, prevailed on the convention to ratify the "constitution on his personal pledge to obtain the amendment" desired. After Madison made this pledge the constitution was ratified by a majority of 8 in a vote of 168.[2]

When Madison introduced what is now the First Amendment's religion clauses, there were several basic nationwide concerns. One dealt with the fact that the states retained rights pertaining to certain issues such as religion and education. The Constitution was therefore dealing with issues of concern to the federal government because there was a strong conviction that the United States were a federal but not a national government. This was spelled out in the Tenth Amendment in the Bill of Rights.

The second issue was liberty of conscience or the free exercise of religion because states with established religions had a history of persecution and restriction of nonconformists. The third issue was that of laws dealing with government endorsement and support of religion and with religious control of government, which were aspects of state establishments of religion. Alexander Hamilton of New York, who played such a large part in the formation of the Union, has provided one of the few contemporary definitions of an established religion. In his "Remarks on the Quebec Bill" in 1775 he referred to "a certain writer" who defined "an established religion" as "a religion which the civil authority engages not only to protect, but to support."[3]

The chief political debate at the time the First Amendment was adopted was not between those who wanted to support religion and those who didn't. It had already been decided in the Constitutional Convention not to give the federal government any power to deal with religion. The problem faced by the first Congress was one of defining a prohibition so that no future Congress would assume an authority that had not been granted under the Constitution. Madison tried to deal with these various issues in proposing the following amendment: "The civil rights of none shall be abridged on account of religious belief or worship, nor shall any national religion be established, nor shall the full and equal rights of conscience be in any manner, or on any pretext, infringed."[4]

Madison's reference to a national religion was rejected in committee. It had been referred on July 21, 1789, to a committee of eleven members, one from each state, with Madison representing Virginia. On August 15 that committee reported to the House the following: "no religion shall be established by law nor shall the equal rights of conscience be infringed."[5] Madison evidently was persuaded that the committee's deletion of the word "national" was appropriate, for in his first remarks in the August 15 debate he said in referring to the committee statement: "he thought it as well expressed as the nature of the language would admit."[6]

However, Madison again proposed the word "national" after Representative Samuel Huntington of Connecticut feared that private agreements to support churches on the state level would be unenforceable in federal courts as establishments of religion. The following excerpts from the debate begin with Madison's comment on Huntington's point and also reveal what happened to the word "national."

Mr. MADISON thought, if the word national was inserted before religion, it would satisfy the minds of honorable gentlemen. He believed that the people feared one sect might obtain a pre-eminence, or two combine together, and establish a religion to which they would compel others to conform. He thought if the word national was introduced, it would point the amendment directly to the object it was intended to prevent.

Mr. LIVERMORE was not satisfied with that amendment; but he did not wish them to dwell long on the subject. He thought it would be better if it was altered, and made to read in this manner, that Congress shall make no laws touching religion, or infringing the rights of conscience.

Mr. GERRY did not like the term national, proposed by the gentleman from Virginia, and he hoped it would not be adopted by the House. . . .

Mr. MADISON withdrew his motion, but observed that the words "no national religion shall be established by law," did not imply that the Government was a national one; the question was then taken on Livermore's motion, and passed in the affirmative 31 for, and 20 against it.[7]

Livermore's motion, however, was changed before being sent to the Senate. Fisher Ames of Massachusetts moved the following language: "Congress shall make no law establishing religion, or to prevent the free exercise thereof, or to infringe the rights of conscience."[8] On August 25 the House sent the amendment to the Senate, requesting its concurrence.

The Senate debate on the House amendment began on September 3, but no record of the debate exists. However, we have the following record of the September 3 proceedings:

The resolve of the House of Representatives . . . was read, as followeth:

"Art. III. Congress shall make no law establishing religion, or prohibiting the free exercise thereof; nor shall the rights of conscience be infringed."

The Senate resumed the consideration of the resolve of the House . . .

On motion to amend Article the third, and to strike out these words:

"Religion, or prohibiting the free exercise thereof," and insert "one religious sect or society in preference to others":

It passed in the negative. (In the language of the day, it was defeated.)

On motion for reconsideration:

It passed in the affirmative.

On motion that Article the third be stricken out:

It passed in the negative.

On motion to adopt the following, in lieu of the third Article: "Congress shall not make any law infringing the rights of conscience, or establishing any religious sect or society":

It passed in the negative.

On motion to amend the third Article, to read thus: "Congress shall make no law establishing any particular denomination or religion in preference to another, or prohibiting the free exercise thereof, nor shall the rights of conscience be infringed":

It passed in the negative.

On the question upon the third Article as it came from the House of Representatives:

It passed in the negative.

On motion to adopt the third Article proposed in the resolve of the House of Representatives, amended by striking out these words, "Nor shall the rights of conscience be infringed":

It passed in the affirmative.[9]

These actions clearly show that Congress was not prepared to accept a proposal that merely prevented preferential treatment of one denomination over others or a proposal that merely prevented the establishment of one religious sect. It rejected the idea that establishment means preferment.

When the Senate on September 9 again took up the House amendment it was changed to read: "Congress shall make no law establishing articles of faith or a mode of worship, or prohibiting the free exercise of religion. . . ."[10]

The House rejected the Senate's proposal with respect to religion and proposed a joint conference committee, which was acceptable to the Senate. In the compromise between the Senate and House versions of various amendments proposed for the Bill of Rights, the House conferees, and subsequently the House, agreed to accept the Senate amendments provided that the Senate accept the following language for what is now the First Amendment: "Congress shall make no law respecting an establishment of religion or prohibiting the free exercise thereof; or abridging the freedom of speech, or of the press; or the right of the people peaceably to assemble, and petition the government for a redress of grievances."[11]

These compromises were accepted by the House on September 24, 1789, and by the Senate on September 25. The language of the First Amendment as clarified by the House debate and the Senate's motions that preceded its adoption contribute to our understanding of separation of church and state. The First Amendment clause, "Congress shall make no law respecting an establishment of religion," means what it says. The word "respecting" means concerning or touching upon, or in relation to, or with regard to. The word "establishment" had at least two meanings at the time the First

Amendment was adopted and has those meanings today. One was a technical reference to monopoly status, such as the Roman Catholic church had for many years in Spain; or to government patronage and control of a church, such as the Church of England; or government regulation and financial support of one or more churches, as in some colonies and states in early America.

The other meaning of the word "establishment" is *institution*. The two meanings are used interchangeably today as they were then. A religious establishment is an institution of religion. Madison spoke of "the *establishment* of the chaplainship" in Congress.[12] He vetoed a bill to give a parcel of land to a Baptist church with the statement that "Congress shall make no law respecting a religious establishment."[13] Jefferson, in drafting a "Bill for the Establishment of District Colleges and University" and in the Regulations of the University of Virginia, provided that the students "will be free and expected to attend religious worship at the *establishment* of their respective sects."[14] Whether either or both of these definitions apply, it is clear that the amendment does not say "Congress shall make no law establishing religion," but does say "no law *respecting* an establishment of religion." It therefore cannot be construed as authorizing Congress to support religious institutions.

It would be illogical to suppose that an amendment expressly designed to prohibit a power never given to Congress in the Constitution should be construed as creating the authority to enact laws benefitting religion financially. Yet this is precisely what contemporary proponents of aid to churches are trying to do. The U.S. Catholic Conference (USCC), as indicated in an earlier chapter, filed in 1983 a "friend of the court" brief in the Supreme Court with respect to *Mueller* v. *Allen* in an effort to reinterpret the Establishment Clause as an authorization of financial benefits for churches. Among the arguments in that brief are the following:

(1) "The phrase 'respecting an establishment' cannot mean concerning or touching upon religion. Indeed that was the terminology of Livermore's proposal which was eventually rejected." Actually, the Livermore motion was only temporarily replaced by another because it triumphed in the final vote; the phrase "touching upon" was replaced by the word "respecting," which means the same thing. It is reasonable to suppose that Fisher Ames's motion that temporarily replaced Livermore's "Congress shall make no law establishing religion" was intended to make sure that there was a reference to establishment in the motion. The Ames and Livermore motions were united in the final wording in the phrase "respecting an establishment of religion."

(2) The USCC brief also says: "The language of the clause does not concern itself with religion in general, but with the particular problem of an *establishment* of religion. There was no concern expressed during the August 15 debate that Congress might enact a law beneficial to religion or religious institutions."[15] This argument overlooks the fact that the entire debate was about establishments of religion and the further fact that there were no establishments of religion in the United States or the colonies apart from laws intending to provide financial and other benefits to religion and religious institutions.

(3) The third argument of the USCC brief is that the word *establishment* really means preferment. It said: "Nothing in the House and Senate proceedings suggests that the thrust

of the compromise differs in any material degree from the final House and Senate versions. It was directed against the preferment or establishment of religion." Actually, there are crucial differences between the final product and the House and Senate versions. One crucial difference is the use of the word "respecting." A second difference is that the final Senate version dealt only with "articles of faith or a mode of worship," whereas an establishment of religion also includes religious education, church finances, and medical, charitable, and other enterprises of churches.

The USCC brief and the position of the bishops is that the First Amendment is against preferential aid to churches, not against aid as such. Yet, the Senate votes were exactly contrary to the USCC statement about preferment. When the Senate rejected the idea that establishment is preferment by voting against all attempts to limit the meaning of establishment to the concept of preference, it did not thereby imply that nonpreferential aid is acceptable. No consideration was ever given to nonpreferential aid to religion because the First Amendment is not an act of empowerment, but an act of denying Congress any power to vote laws respecting an establishment of religion.

Over the years of discussion of the meaning of the First Amendment, two schools of thought have emerged. One school selects statements from some early leaders in government to conclude that the First Amendment was intended only to prohibit a single national establishment of religion and, therefore, the Constitution permits nonpreferential aid to religion. The problems in drawing such a conclusion can be summarized as follows:

(1) At the time the Constitution was adopted, it con-

ferred no power on Congress to make any law respecting religious matters. The First Amendment did not change that or by implication grant Congress any right to intervene in religious matters.

(2) The only attempt in the first Congress to propose a prohibition on a single national establishment of religion was rejected in committee and repudiated on the floor of the House. The author of the proposal withdrew it, and the House then adopted a motion that "Congress shall make no laws touching religion. . . ."

(3) The Senate rejected the idea of merely banning preferential treatment or establishing "one religious sect or society in preference to another."

(4) At the time the First Amendment was adopted, the primary public controversy about state establishments, in the only states where any establishment existed, was that of taxing people to support ministers, teachers of religion, and churches. This had been the issue not only in single establishment colonies and states like Virginia, but in multiple establishment states. Single establishment states either eliminated establishment over this issue of government funding of religion, or tried to preserve religious funding by providing it to a number of churches. Taxation for religious purposes was under such attack even in multiple establishment states that it was simply a matter of time before it would be ended everywhere. No one proposed multiple or nonpreferential taxation or funding for religion on the federal level. The First Amendment, in forbidding Congress to make any law "respecting an establishment of religion," cannot be construed as authorizing taxation for or financial aid to any religious group, as some contemporary church pressure groups imply.

(5) When the Bill of Rights and the Constitution were adopted, those who framed these documents did not list everything they meant by the word *establishment*. It is obvious from various inherited practices and various statements of government leaders that some opposed and some supported government chaplaincies or prayer at public events or Thanksgiving proclamations or other religious activities. There was, however, a context for the First Amendment that was not disputed. That context includes the following: (a) religious liberty and equality for all religious expression rather than mere toleration of minority groups; (b) no federal governmental support for religious organizations in general or Christianity or Protestantism or any other sectarian emphasis with respect to the people of the United States; (c) government intervention in religious matters was left solely to the states, but that intervention was limited by Article VI, Section 3; (d) the federal government was to protect and not infringe the free exercise of religion or its crucial element, conscience; and (e) no church or combination of churches would be permitted to control or direct the federal government. The essence of establishment was the ability of churches to command government support, as there was no effort by the federal government to dictate church policy. Any government effort to control churches would run into the free exercise guarantee.

The second school of thought with respect to the First Amendment holds that the Constitution and the First Amendment must be construed as giving the government no power whatsoever to aid or to inhibit religion. It is to be neutral with respect to religious matters, except that it must guarantee to everyone religious liberty and the free exercise of religion.

This leaves the raising of money, the winning of adherents, and the determining of doctrines, programs, church government, and all other religious matters to each religious body.

The chief problem with this understanding of the First Amendment is the Congress and the executive branch have always been subject to pressures to support this or that religious expression or to appropriate money in aid of church projects. Some early presidents and members of Congress have been more strict in their adherence to separation of church and state than others. This was understandable because the idea of separation of church and state was revolutionary. There was no previous pattern and no blueprint for such separation. It was an idea that existed more clearly in the minds of some, such as Roger Williams, James Madison, and Thomas Jefferson, than in others. But even those men found no occasion to list every possible violation or argue every implication. They also tended to focus on certain major problems in order to accomplish their chief objectives rather than to fight every existing practice.

Some early religious practices remain and are ignored, as is evident in the nonattendance of members of the House and Senate for the daily opening prayer of the chaplains. Some, like the annual proclamation of Thanksgiving, have lost their religious import and signal a basically secular holiday. Others have been eliminated by Congress or otherwise changed. Over the years since the idea of separation of church and state was proclaimed there has been continuing pressure by some churches or their leaders to alter it. But there has also been continuing devotion to the idea by a majority of Jews, Protestants, Roman Catholics, and the unchurched.

Some proponents of government aid to churches indicate

that Congress could not have intended a prohibition of aid to religion because so many of the "founding fathers" violated this prohibition at one point or another. The thesis of this and the following chapter is that Congress did intend to preclude any government support of or interference with religion, that there were violations of this because of the colonial inheritance or practice, and that the doctrine of separation of church and state was the beginning of a revolution against "establishment" rather than an abrupt consummation of disestablishment.

NOTES

1. *Annals of the Congress of the United States* (Washington: Gales and Seaton, 1834), vol. 1, p. 730; hereafter *Annals.*
2. Sanford H. Cobb, p. 508.
3. Anson Phelps Stokes, vol. 1, p. 510.
4. *Annals,* vol. 1, p. 434.
5. Ibid., p. 729.
6. Ibid., p. 730.
7. Ibid., p. 731.
8. Ibid., p. 766.
9. *Journal of the First Session of the Senate* . . . (Washington: Gales and Seaton, 1820), p. 70.
10. Ibid., p. 77.
11. Ibid., p. 87.
12. Leo Pfeffer, *Church, State, and Freedom* (Boston: Beacon Press, 1953), p. 140; emphasis added.
13. Ibid.
14. Ibid.
15. Emphasis added.

CHAPTER IV

The Revolution Against Establishment

Separation of church and state has to be understood in at least three dimensions. It is a result of the fact that the Constitution grants no power to the federal government to become involved in religious matters. It is also a result of the First Amendment, which forbids United States interference in the field of religion. In addition, it is a product of a continuing revolution that was launched in the colonies and has continued through much of American history. That revolution includes at least the following five developments.

RELIGIOUS ACTS

When the Constitution was developed, a number of states had religious tests for voting and holding public office. Pennsylvania required an officeholder to believe in one God and in a future state of rewards and punishments. New York excluded all Catholics from state office. New Jersey allowed "every privilege and immunity" only to Protestants. The constitutions of Maryland, New Hampshire, North Carolina, and Vermont contained provisions barring all but Protestants from the right to vote and hold office.[1]

The states were not obligated under the Constitution to eliminate these tests. The reference to Article VI, Section 3, to religious tests is "as a qualification to any office or public trust under the United States." Nevertheless, over a period of years the original states eliminated their religious tests for public office or ignored them. The Delaware Constitution of 1792 used the same wording as the federal Constitution, but made it applicable "under this state."[2] Rhode Island never had a religious test, and in its first constitution, adopted in 1842, specifically banned any test.[3] New Hampshire in 1852 removed from its constitution of 1792 the relic of a Protestant requirement for senators and representatives.[4] Some states took longer. New Jersey, for example, did not change its constitution until the twentieth century.[5]

Vermont was admitted to the Union in 1791, and in 1793 dropped all religious tests.[6] In 1796, a part of the "Territories of the United States South of the Ohio" became the state of Tennessee. Although Congress made no specific requirement about religious freedom in admitting Tennessee, the state constitution in Article XI, Section 4, used the federal formula in banning religious tests.[7]

It is significant that every state in the Union has abandoned religious tests for voting and for holding public office, or has never had such tests.

RELIGIOUS TAXES

A crucial aspect of state disestablishment of churches was the people's revolt against taxation for religious purposes. This use of their funds was the chief point at which establishment touched them.

In Virginia there was a long struggle against establishment, led by dissenting churches and such persons as Thomas Jefferson, James Madison, and George Mason. The result was a Bill for Establishing Religious Freedom (1785), which, in its long preamble, included these words: "... that to compel a man to furnish contributions of money for the propagation of opinions which he disbelieves, is sinful and tyrannical; that even the forcing him to support this or that teacher of his own religious persuasion, is depriving him of the comfortable liberty of giving his contributions to the particular pastor whose morals he would make his pattern. . . ."[8]

The preamble was followed by these words: "We, the General Assembly, do enact, that no man shall be compelled to frequent or support any religious worship, place, or ministry whatsoever, nor shall be enforced, restrained, molested or burdened in his body or goods, nor shall otherwise suffer on account of his religious opinions or belief. . . ."[9]

The New Jersey Constitution of 1776 said: "nor shall any person within this colony, ever be obliged to pay tithes, taxes or any other rates, for the purpose of building or repairing any other church or churches, place or places of worship, or for the maintenance of any minister or ministry, contrary to what he believes to be right or has deliberately or voluntarily engaged himself to perform."[10] The Pennsylvania Constitution of 1776 had a similar provision that no one "can be compelled to attend any religious worship, or erect or support any place of worship, or maintain any ministry, contrary to, or against, his own free will and consent."[11]

The Georgia Constitution of 1777 provided that no one shall, "unless by consent, support any teacher or teachers except those of their own profession. The Georgia Constitution of 1798 contained an even stronger statement against any person paying "tithes, taxes, or any other rate" for religious purposes unless he "hath voluntarily engaged to do so."[12] Vermont, which drafted a constitution in 1777 and affirmed it in 1779 and 1782, had a similar statement against compulsory support of religion.[13]

The South Carolina Constitution of 1778 said that "No persons shall, by law, be obliged to pay towards the maintenance and support of a religious worship that he does not freely join in, or has not voluntarily engaged to support." At this time, South Carolina still had a system of "multiple establishments of all Protestant denominations, but its constitution of 1790 eliminated all vestiges of establishment.[14]

Rhode Island never had any religious assessments and forbade the practice of government funding of churches. Delaware, in its constitution of 1792, had a provision against religious taxation that was virtually identical with that of Pennsylvania.[15] When Kentucky was admitted to the Union in 1791, its constitution had a similar provision against compulsory religious support.[16] Massachusetts in 1831 gave up its multiple establishments of religion, and in its constitution of 1833 made all religious expenses the responsibility of "the several religious societies of this Commonwealth. . . ."[17]

This virtually unanimous growth of opposition in the early states of the Union to taxation and public funding of religion is further evidence of the revolution for separation of church and state. Virginia did not start the revolution, as some writers have implied. It was an indigenous revolt in each colony and state. However, Virginia's Statute of Religious Liberty (1786) was the best statement of separation of church and state, probably because it was written by Thomas Jefferson. It has, therefore, become the literary and intellectual example for other states to follow.

THE FIRST AMENDMENT AND THE STATES

When the U.S. Constitution was ratified, only the states were empowered to deal with religion. However, in 1868, following the Civil War, the Constitution was amended so as to make the First Amendment, and in fact the first eight amendments, applicable to the various states. The Fourteenth Amendment contains the following statement: "No state shall make or enforce any law which shall abridge the privileges and immunities of citizens of the United States, nor shall any state deprive any person of life, liberty or property without due process of law. . . ."

During the congressional discussion of the proposed Fourteenth Amendment, the amendment's floor manager, Senator J. M. Howard (R-Mich.), stated in explaining it, that "to these privileges and immunities . . . should be added the personal rights guaranteed and secured by the first eight amendments to the Constitution." He also said: "The great object of the first section of the amendment is, therefore, to restrain the power of the states and compel them at all times to respect these fundamental guarantees."[18]

In similar fashion, the House of Representatives understood that the purpose of the Fourteenth Amendment was to make the Bill of Rights applicable to the states. Rep. John Bingham (R-Ohio), who was called by Justice Hugo Black "the Madison of the Fourteenth Amendment," stated that the amendment was intended to overturn *Barron* v. *Baltimore* (1833), in which the Supreme Court had held that the Bill of Rights was not applicable to the states.[19] The Supreme Court, however, did not readily accept this legislative history and, hence, did not make the Establishment Clause applicable to the states until the 1940s. In fact, the Supreme Court has at times been reluctant to defend separation of church and state, not only in terms of the Establishment Clause, but also with respect to the free exercise of conscience, as we shall see in Chapters V and VI.

After repeatedly refusing to apply the Fourteenth Amendment to the Bill of Rights, the Court, in *Cantwell* v. *Connecticut* (1940),[20] decided that the religion clauses of the First Amendment, especially the Free Exercise Clause, were applicable to the states via the Fourteenth Amendment. The *Cantwell* case, raised by Jehovah's Witnesses, involved a state statute that required a certificate of authorization to solicit funds for religious, charitable, or philanthropic causes. The Court unanimously decided that the statute was unconstitutional.

The Court said: "The First Amendment declares that Congress shall make no law respecting an establishment of religion or prohibiting the free exercise thereof. The Fourteenth Amendment has rendered the legislatures of the states as incompetent as Congress to enact such laws."

In 1947, in *Everson* v. *Board of Education of Ewing Township, N.J.,*[21] the Supreme Court specifically made the Establishment Clause applicable to the states and spelled out its meaning:

> The "establishment of religion" clause of the First Amendment means at least this:
>
> Neither a state nor the Federal Government can set up a church.
>
> Neither can pass laws which aid one religion, aid all religions, or prefer one religion over another.
>
> Neither can force nor influence a person to go to or

remain away from church against his will or force him to
profess a belief or disbelief in any religion.

No person can be punished for entertaining or professing
religious beliefs or disbeliefs, for church attendance or nonattendance.

No tax in any amount, large or small, can be levied to
support any religious activities or institutions, whatever they
may be called, or whatever form they may adopt to teach or
practice religion.

Neither a state nor the Federal Government can, openly
or secretly, participate in the affairs of any religious organizations or groups and vice versa.

In the words of Jefferson, the clause against establishment of religion by law was intended to erect a "wall of
separation between Church and State."

What the Court said was better than what the Court
permitted, as we shall see in the next chapter, because the
Court actually ruled in favor of reimbursing parents for the
cost of bus transportation to church schools. However, the
fact that the Supreme Court has now applied the First
Amendment to the states is a part of the continuing revolution set in motion by the Constitutional Convention and by
earlier achievements in the colonies. The Court has also contributed to the advance of separation of church and state in
some of its decisions, even though it has not maintained
Jefferson's "wall of separation between church and state."

PUBLIC SCHOOLS

In colonial America all education was generally religious and,
for the most part, conducted under church auspices. The first

compulsory education law was adopted in Massachusetts in 1642. In 1647, public education became the responsibility of every township of 50 or more householders. In every town of 100 or more householders, a grammar school was to be set up. These schools, although maintained by the town, were, during the colonial period, under the supervision of the minister.[22] Outside of New England the schools were private or parochial and either supported by the rich or by local churches or, in establishment colonies, by the church tax.

After the war with England was over, but before the Constitution was adopted, the Continental Congress adopted a Northwest Ordinance in 1785 that ʻlaid down the general principles of the American territorial system. The Northwest Territory was made up of western lands between the Mississippi River, the Ohio River, and the Great Lakes.

The congressional ordinance of 1785 had ordered a rectangular system of townships with provisions that "reserved the lot No. 16 of every township, for the maintenance of public schools within the said township. . . ." Lot 16 and each other lot included 640 acres. Lot No. 29 was for the support of religion. This policy was begun in Ohio in 1786.[23] However, the Congressional Committee, in considering this, removed support for religion from the Ordinance of 1785. Nevertheless, the Massachusetts-dominated Ohio Company lobbied through Congress a grant to implement the system.[24]

The Northwest Ordinance of 1787 was continued by Act of Congress, August 7, 1789, but support for religion was not in the Ordinance of 1787 or its renewal. The Ordinance of 1787, however, contained the following reference to education and religion:

Article I. No person, demeaning himself in a peaceable and orderly manner, shall ever be molested on account of his mode of worship, or religious sentiments, in the said territory. . . .

Article III. Religion, morality and knowledge, being necessary to good government and the happiness of mankind, schools and the means of education shall forever be encouraged. . . .[25]

The first state to be carved out of the Northwest Territory, Ohio, adopted a constitution in 1802 that provided that "each and every denomination of religious societies in each surveyed township, which now is or may hereafter be formed in the State," shall receive "an equal participation, according to their number of adherents, of the profits arising from the land granted by Congress for the support of religion, agreeably to the ordinance or act of Congress making the appropriation."[26] Congress, in admitting Ohio to the Union in 1803, did not require a change in the state constitution or practice, evidently mindful of the fact that education as well as religion were left to the states under the federal Constitution.

It was not until 1860 that Ohio decided that school funds from the earlier sale of congressional grants for education could be used only for the "State University" in the case of higher education and only for "common schools" so as to prevent their use for sectarian institutions.[27]

Subsequently, President Ulysses S. Grant in his Seventh Annual Message (December 7, 1875) asked Congress to adopt a new amendment to the Constitution that would require the

states to establish and forever maintain free public schools
. . . for all children . . . irrespective of sex, color, birthplace
or religion; forbidding the teaching in said schools of religious, atheistic, or pagan tenets; and prohibiting the granting
of any school funds or school taxes . . . for the benefit or in
aid, directly or indirectly, of any religious sect or denomination. . . .[28]

Grant's proposal was, with some modification, introduced in the House and adopted by a vote of 180 for and 7
against, with 98 not voting.[29] The Senate Judiciary Committee considered various substitutes and amendments to the
House resolution and proposed its own amendment, which
embodied Grant's recommendation. The Senate vote was 28
for, 16 against, and 27 absent or not voting. It failed to get
the necessary two-thirds majority to submit it to the states.
The reasons for this included the feeling that it was unnecessary, given existing constitutional guarantees; that the various
states should make their own decisions; and that it was too
divisive an issue in the aftermath of a divisive Civil War.
There was also strong Roman Catholic opposition.[30]

Although Grant's proposal, sometimes known as the
Blaine amendment because of its sponsor in the Senate, did
not enter the federal Constitution, it came into effect by
another route. Every state admitted to the Union since 1876
was required by Congress to provide constitutionally for a
public school system "free from sectarian control."[31]

It is also noteworthy that such states as Illinois, Michigan, and Wisconsin, formed from territories governed by the
Northwest Ordinance and admitted to the Union before the
congressional requirement, have adopted constitutional provisions either against sectarian instruction in public schools

or against public property or funds being used for sectarian purposes. The Fourteenth Amendment, and hence the First Amendment, also apply to the whole nation.

This does not mean that there has not been a continuing struggle by churches for support of religious schools. That struggle arose as a result of efforts to eliminate sectarian religion from the public schools. In 1827, the Massachusetts legislature, having to deal with a number of different religious sects, decided that textbooks could not be used in the public schools if they favored "any religious sect or tenet." It was sectarianism, rather than religion as such, that was to be avoided. The first impetus toward ending sectarianism came from Protestants, but the net result was a vague Protestantism that left neither Protestants nor Roman Catholics happy.[32]

In looking for a way to continue their religious education, many Protestants turned to the Sunday school, which had existed before but without quite the same centrality it assumed in the nineteenth century. Other Protestants began to explore weekday church schools, such as the elementary schools the Lutherans in Pennsylvania established.[33] In the 1840s, Presbyterians began to organize parochial schools and, in New Jersey, worked with little success to get public funds to support them. Faced with the difficulty of financing a system of parochial schools, the Presbyterians abandoned them about 1870.[34]

Because the public schools included some religious practices such as Bible reading and prayer that were largely Protestant in nature, the Roman Catholic church was concerned about their effect on Roman Catholic children. A Roman Catholic council held in Baltimore in 1840 directed priests to do what they could to eliminate those religious practices from the public schools. In the course of their political efforts to establish a genuinely secular public school system, Protestants rallied to the support of public schools as they then existed.[35]

As a consequence, Bishop John Hughes of New York City asked for a share of the Public School Society's fund for Roman Catholic schools. He also petitioned New York City for a "proportion of the funds appropriated for the common schools. . . ." After a public hearing, the Board of Aldermen voted 15 to 1 against the request.[36] The legislature in 1842 also refused public funds for parochial schools. In 1844, the state legislature enacted a law that said that "no school shall be entitled to a portion of the school moneys in which the religious sectarian doctrine or tenet of any particular Christian or other religious sect shall be taught, inculcated or practiced. . . ."[37]

Later, in 1894, the state constitution, in Article 9, Section 4, prohibited the state or any subdivision thereof from using "its property or credit or any public money . . . directly or indirectly, in aid or maintenance . . . of any school or institution of learning wholly or in part under the control or direction of any religious denomination or in which any denominational tenet or doctrine is taught." It also prohibits the teaching of "any denominational tenet" in the public schools.[38]

Although the revolution against public funding of religious schools seems to have been won in the various states, there have been and are continuing counter-revolutionary efforts by the Roman Catholic bishops, who have never fully accepted the American doctrine of separation of church and state, and from some Protestant denominations, such as the Christian Reformed church and the Missouri Synod Lutherans, whose leaders seek support for their parochial schools.

THE CHURCHES, THE STATE, AND INDIANS

One of the arguments sometimes used against separation of church and state is that the Congress that adopted the First Amendment did not intend to deny aid to religious institutions or it would not have sanctioned aid for missions to the Indians. There were apparently two reasons for such aid. One was related to the view of government leaders that the Indians were citizens of foreign nations and, hence, subject to their own laws rather than to the Constitution. The United States, therefore, negotiated treaties with the Indian nations. President Washington, for example, in 1795 concluded a treaty with the Oneida, Tuscarora, and Stockbridge Indians under which the U.S. provided $1,000 to build a church at Oneida in place of the one the British burned during the war.[39] The use of treaties to bypass the First Amendment is not constitutionally valid, although it seems to have been used a number of times to aid religious enterprises in Indian territory.

The second and major reason for providing money for religious activity among the Indians was related to U.S. military policy. Although there had been Christian missionary activity among the Indians during the colonial period, the new nation assisted missionaries for reasons of national security. The first Secretary of War, Henry Knox, largely shaped U.S. policy toward the Indians. He believed that costly and bloody wars with the Indians could be avoided by civilizing them. Knox and President Washington wanted "missionaries to reside in the [Indian] nation . . . teaching them the great duties of religion and morality, and to inculcate a friendship and attachment to the United States."[40] Knox, however, forbade the teaching of Christianity to those not yet converted, and sought instead to send teachers and farmers to help them establish farms.[41]

Congress in 1819 established a permanent "Civilization Fund" from which missionaries were paid. One of the purposes of using religion was to conclude hostilities with Indians who had assisted the British against the United States. Schools were also established in Indian lands where, in some cases, missionaries were teachers.

The government assigned Christian denominations to specific Indian groups or agencies to avoid competition within the agency. There was no controversy about such comity arrangements or spheres of influence between Protestant groups, but some missionary boards objected to the Roman Catholic church's control of too many Indian agencies. "Behind the opposition to Roman Catholic missionaries in many cases was resentment by both agents and missionaries when priests forbade children to attend government or mission schools."[42]

The conflict came to a head after it was revealed that the government in a period of eight years ending in 1893 had given Catholic schools $2,355,416 out of a total of $3,767,951 for all schools, including nonchurch schools. Eight Protestant agencies had together received a total of only $938,977. The Protestant Episcopal church, the Methodist Episcopal church, the Presbyterians, and the American Missionary

Association in 1892 refused other subsidies and began political action against the discriminatory aid.[43]

Congress cut financial aid in 1895, and in 1897 decided that "it is to be the settled policy of the government to hereafter make no appropriation for education in any sectarian school."[44]

Both Jefferson and Madison had indicated that the best enforcement of separation of church and state lay in the opposing religious interests of the various churches. Before the Virginia Convention in 1788, Madison answered the question: "Is a bill of rights a security for" religious liberty? He said:

> If there were a majority of one sect, a bill of rights would be a poor protection for liberty. Happily for the [United States] they enjoy the utmost freedom of religion. This freedom arises from the multiplicity of sects, which pervades America and which is the best and only security for religious liberty in any society. For where there is such a variety of sects there cannot be a majority of any one sect to oppress and persecute the rest.[45]

In other words, what Madison thought of as a kind of built-in enforcement mechanism persuaded Congress in 1897 to implement the First Amendment with respect to subsidies for Indian missions. This sustains our thesis that the American idea of separation of church and state was not fully implemented when the Constitution and the Bill of Rights were adopted. Instead, it was a revolutionary idea that has increasingly won acceptance from the American people in spite of the pressures from politicians and church hierarchies for government aid.

The fact that elected government officials did not faithfully obey the Constitution does not mean that the Constitution thereby loses its validity and that the courts are subsequently estopped from enforcing the First Amendment.

NOTES

1. Stokes, vol. 1, p. 274, pp. 427-444.
2. Ibid., p. 437.
3. Ibid., p. 443.
4. Ibid., p. 431.
5. Ibid., p. 436.
6. Ibid., p. 442.
7. Ibid., p. 404.
8. Ibid., pp. 392-393.
9. Ibid., p. 393.
10. Ibid., p. 435.
11. Ibid., p. 438.
13. Ibid., p. 441.
14. Ibid., p. 433-434.
15. Ibid., p. 437.
16. Ibid., p. 445.
17. Ibid., p. 426.
18. *Congressional Globe*, 39th Congress, 1st Session, p. 2765.
19. Ibid., pp. 1088-90. See also *Congressional Globe*, 42nd Congress, 1st Session, Appendix, p. 150, where Bingham restated his intention in drafting the Fourteenth Amendment.
20. 310 U.S. 296.
21. 330 U.S. 1.
22. Pfeffer, pp. 276-277.
23. Ibid., p. 279; Stokes, vol. 1, p. 481.
24. Ronald A. Smith, "Freedom of Religion and the Land Ordinance of 1785," *Journal of Church and State,* vol. 24, no. 3, Autumn 1982; Commager, p. 128.
25. Commager, p. 128.
26. Stokes, vol. 1, p. 481.
27. Ibid.

28. Elwyn A. Smith, *Religious Liberty in the United States* (Philadelphia: Fortress Press, 1972), p. 117.

29. Stokes, vol. II, p. 723.

30. Ibid., p. 727.

31. Pfeffer, p. 131.

32. John M. Swomley Jr., *Religion, The State and the Schools* (New York: Pegasus, 1968), p. 62.

33. Ibid., pp. 62-63.

34. Lewis J. Sherrill, *Presbyterian Parochial Schools 1841-1870* (New Haven: Yale University Press, 1932).

35. Swomley, p. 63; Mary Perkins Ryan, *Are Parochial Schools the Answer* (New York: Holt, Rinehart and Winston, 1964), pp. 33-34.

36. Pfeffer, pp. 434-444.

37. Ibid., p. 444.

38. Ibid., p. 444-445.

39. Robert L. Cord, *Separation of Church and State* (New York: Lambeth Press, 1982), p. 58.

40. R. Pierce Beaver, *Church, State and the American Indians* (St. Louis: Concordia Publishing House, 1966), pp. 64-65.

41. Ibid., p. 66.

42. Ibid., p. 159.

43. Ibid., p. 167.

44. Ibid., pp. 167-168.

45. Gaillard Hunt, ed., *Writings of James Madison* (New York: G. P. Putnam's Sons, 1900-1909), vol. V, p. 176.

CHAPTER V

The Supreme Court and Separation of Church and State

Any revolution designed to benefit the people must always be wary of counter-revolutionary tendencies that would thwart and reverse the revolution. Separation of church and state in our interpretation is a continuing achievement that was not accomplished once and for all two centuries ago. In general, public opinion, as reflected in state referenda on such issues as tuition tax credits for private religious schools, has supported a clear separation of church and state by rejecting aid to church schools.

The Supreme Court, however, has eroded the doctrine of separation of church and state in a number of cases. The Court has ignored the fact that the Constitution is a bill of powers that gives no power to any government agency to deal with religious matters. The Court has also, again and again, used devices to erode the Establishment Clause's clear prohibition against government involvement with religion. Only in a few cases has it defended the Establishment Clause with clarity.

In an 1899 case, *Bradfield* v. *Roberts* (175 U.S. 291), the Court approved public funds for a Roman Catholic hospital in the District of Columbia on the ground that "it is simply the case of a secular corporation being managed by people who hold to the doctrines of the Roman Catholic church.

. . ." In other words, the Court rationalized government funding of religious institutions by claiming a secular purpose. Church hospitals and other church institutions are a part of the mission of the church. However, the Court in effect said that, if the members of a church use a secular corporation to manage church institutions to promote a church's mission, the religious aspect is secondary and constitutes no breach of the Establishment Clause.

In 1930, in *Cochran v. Louisiana State Board of Education* (281 U.S. 370), the Court permitted the state to provide secular textbooks to parochial school pupils in spite of a state constitutional provision that "no money shall ever be taken from the public treasury directly or indirectly in aid of any church, sect, or denomination of religion." Textbooks are as essential to sectarian instruction as buildings and teachers, yet the Court ruled that they benefitted children and aided education and literacy in the state. Not only did the Court ignore the fact that the state constitution banned any aid, but it also ignored the religious, educational, and organizational unity of the school to assert that the government could directly finance a single component of religious education so long as it could be deemed secular.

In the *Everson* case in 1947, the Court permitted the State of New Jersey to reimburse parents of parochial school pupils for money spent by them for transportation to church schools on regular buses operated by the public transportation system. The Court reasoned that the state was not benefitting the school, but individual parents, and was equally benefitting all citizens without regard to religious beliefs. The law, however, did not provide for reimbursement for other private school students. It did not provide for all children to use buses for any health, recreational, or educational purpose, but only for schools. Thus, it was not child benefit, but of benefit to religion as it provided transportation to religious schools.

In the days of neighborhood schools, children walked to school. When bus transportation became available, school districts and churches could build better schools to serve a wider geographical area. By building fewer consolidated schools, they could save money. The school bus that made this possible is actually a direct benefit to the school and not to the pupil.

In 1948, in *McCollum* v. *Board of Education* (333 U.S. 203), the decision was clearly in harmony with separation of church and state. The Court decided that the arrangement was unconstitutional whereby public schools permitted children to be released for religious educational purposes on public school property under the compulsory attendance provisions. Justice Black held in his opinion that the state was not only using "tax supported public school buildings . . . for the dissemination of religious doctrines," but "the State also affords sectarian groups an invaluable aid in that it helps to provide pupils for their religious classes through use of the State's compulsory public school machinery. This is not separation of church and state."

A few years later in *Zorach* v. *Clauson* (343 U.S. 306; 1952), the Court permitted "pupils compelled by law to go to school for secular education" to be "released for an hour on condition that they attend religious classes."[1] The religious classes were off the premises of the public school. The Court held that the state could cooperate "with religious authorities by adjusting the schedule of public events to sectarian needs."

Not only did this violate the Establishment Clause, but Justice William O. Douglas in the decision made the unfortunate statement that "we are a religious people whose institutions presuppose a Supreme Being." This defined religion in terms of civil religion, in the sense that religion is useful to American institutions and is, therefore, valid.

In 1961, in *McGowan* v. *Maryland* (366 U.S. 420), the Court ruled that in spite of their historic purpose, compulsory Sunday closing laws are secular in purpose and effect rather than aimed at the advancement of religion. "The Establishment Clause does not ban federal or state regulation of conduct whose reason or effect merely happens to coincide or harmonize with the tenets of some or all religion." Obviously, this decision discriminates against Jews, Seventh Day Adventists, and Seventh Day Baptists for whom Saturday is the Sabbath or day of rest and worship. Thus, it prefers the day of worship of some religious groups over others.

With the prayer cases the Court returned to a separationist position. In *Engel* v. *Vitale* (370 U.S. 421; 1962), the Court abandoned the idea that "we are a religious people" and recognized the rights of parents who dissented even from a general expression of religion. Prior to the *Engel* case, the *Everson, McCollum,* and *Zorach* cases repudiated the notion that the "First Amendment was intended to forbid only government preference of one religion over another, not impartial assistance to all religions." The *Everson* opinion said that "the state [should] be neutral in its relations with groups of religious believers and non-believers."[2] But the *Engel* decision explicitly decided that the state must be neutral between believers and nonbelievers.

In the *Schempp* case (374 U.S. 203; 1963) the Court

banned school devotional exercises and indicated that prayer services were coercive even if children were permitted to leave the room during such services. However, the Court formulated a test that was different from the *Everson* dicta. *Everson* said: "no tax in any amount, large or small, can be levied to support any religious activities or institutions, whatever they may be called, or whatever form they may adopt to teach or practice religion." In *Schempp* the test is this: ". . . to withstand the strictures of the Establishment Clause there must be a secular legislative purpose and a primary effect that neither advances nor inhibits religion." Five years later in *Board of Education* v. *Allen* (392 U.S. 236; 1968) the *Schempp* test was used to validate a law providing secular textbooks for parochial schools.

In 1970 in *Walz* v. *Tax Commission of New York* (397 U.S. 664) and in 1971 in *Lemon* v. *Kurtzman* (403 U.S. 602) the Court added a third test that to be constitutional a statute must not result in "excessive government entanglement with religion."

These three tests were applied in 1971 in *Tilton* v. *Richardson* (403 U.S. 672) to permit government funds to be used for buildings in church colleges in Connecticut. Although neutrality was first set forth as a virtual synonym for separation, it became in *Tilton* a way of permitting government aid to church colleges. In addition to applying the three tests of neutrality, the Court contended that there is a difference between aiding church-related institutions of higher learning and aiding church elementary and secondary schools; namely, that "college students are less impressionable and less subject to religious indoctrination." Such a distinction is artificial and contrived, as there are colleges such as Jerry Falwell's Liberty

Baptist College, Oral Roberts University, and Bob Jones University where opposing religious points of view are not permitted and religious indoctrination is obvious. In *Tilton,* the Court permitted aid even though all four institutions were governed by Catholic religious organizations with faculties and student bodies "predominantly Catholic."

In 1976 in *Roemer* v. *Board of Public Works* (426 U.S. 736) the Court upheld the constitutionality of a Maryland law authorizing an annual subsidy to private, including church, colleges, so long as the state funds were not used for sectarian purposes. The Court found that the colleges involved were not "pervasively sectarian," although a number of classes were begun with prayer, there was religious symbolism, and some teachers wore clerical garb in the classroom. Under this decision, payments of state funds may be made to pay salaries of clergy so long as they are teaching secular subjects. The Supreme Court, in other words, has now established the precedent that religion and theology classes are severable from the rest of a college's activities; that religious symbols and clerical garb in the classroom are not a bar to state aid; and that the reporting to a government agency by the college of its use of the money is not excessive entanglement.

The most serious recent assault on separation of church and state is *Mueller* v. *Allen* (103 S. Ct. 3062; 1983), which validated a Minnesota statute permitting state income taxpayers to claim as an income tax deduction expenses incurred for tuition, textbooks, and transportation in attending elementary and secondary schools. On the surface this may seem to treat the parents of parochial and public schools alike except that tuition, and in most cases transportation and textbooks, are not charged to parents for public schools except in those few instances where students attend a school in another district or have to go elsewhere for a driver's training course. A deduction was also permitted for religious textbooks or books chosen by the parochial schools themselves.

The Minnesota statute spoke of textbooks for "those subjects legally and commonly taught in public elementary and secondary schools." But textbooks may serve the religious purposes of a school by using religious illustrations and examples even though the course title is theoretically the same as history, mathematics, social science, or some other public school subject. Professor George La Noue demonstrated this in his study "Religious Schools and 'Secular' Subjects" in the Summer 1962 *Harvard Educational Review*.

These cases are by no means exhaustive in terms of Supreme Court efforts to find ways of aiding religion financially or symbolically. Among other serious violations of the Constitution are *Lynch* v. *Donnelly* (104 S. Ct. 1355; 1984), which permitted government-sponsored Christian nativity displays, and *Valley Forge Christian College* v. *Americans United For Separation of Church and State* (102 S. Ct. 752; 1982), which permitted the federal government to transfer at no cost a 77-acre tract valued at $1.3 million to an Assembly of God Bible College, which trains people as ministers.

In the *Lynch* case, Chief Justice Burger tried to justify a Christian display with the phrase "we are a religious people," as if Christian and religious are synonymous and Judaism is subordinate. Leo Pfeffer observed that in a listing "of the Supreme Court's most unhappy decisions," headed by *Dred Scott* v. *Sanford, Lynch* v. *Donnelly* must be included because "both are predicated upon the same basic concept: the inherent inferiority of ethnic groups, either because of color of skin or religious commitment."[3]

In several 1985 cases the Court has reaffirmed separation of church and state. One of these, *Grand Rapids School District* v. *Ball,* which was decided by a 5 to 4 vote, involved the sending of public school teachers into parochial or nonpublic schools. The public schools leased and paid for the use of parochial school classrooms. The "shared time" teachers were employees of the public school but, said the Court, "'a significant portion' of them had previously taught in nonpublic schools" and "many of those had been assigned to the same nonpublic school where they were previously employed." In addition, the "public school system apparently provides all of the supplies, material and equipment used in connection with Shared Time instruction" in the parochial schools.

Of the forty-one nonpublic schools involved, forty are identifiably religious. Twenty-eight are Roman Catholic, seven are Christian Reformed, three are Lutheran, one is Seventh Day Adventist, and one is Baptist.

Justice William J. Brennan said in his decision that even a "secular purpose of providing for the education of school children cannot validate government aid to parochial schools when the aid has the effect of promoting a single religion or religion generally or when the aid unduly entangles the government in matters religious." He referred to "the symbolic union of church and state inherent in the provision of secular state-provided public instruction in the religious school buildings" that "threatens to convey a message of state support for religion to students and to the general public."

In a second and "companion" case, *Aguilar* v. *Felton,* the Court, by a similar 5 to 4 vote, invalidated the Title I program administered by New York City. That program was distinguished from the *Grand Rapids* case chiefly because New York City had a system for monitoring the religious content of publicly funded Title I classes in the religious schools. The Court upheld the decision of the U.S. Court of Appeals for the Second Circuit, which had held that "the religious school appears to the public as a joint enterprise staffed with some teachers paid by its religious sponsor and others by the public" (739 F.2d 48, at 67-68).

Justice Brennan noted in his decision that of the Title I students enrolled in private schools 84% were enrolled in Roman Catholic schools and 8% in Hebrew day schools. He indicated that "publicly funded instructors teach classes composed exclusively" of nonpublic school students in private school buildings. He said: "When the state becomes enmeshed with a given denomination in matters of religious significance, the freedom of religious belief of those who are not adherents of that denomination suffers, even when the governmental purpose underlying the involvement is largely secular."

He quoted from *Lemon* v. *Kurtzman* (403 U.S. 602) as follows: "Unlike a book, a teacher cannot be inspected once so as to determine the extent of his or her personal beliefs and subjective acceptance of the limitations imposed by the First Amendment." He referred to "excessive entanglement" in that "agents of the State must visit and inspect the religious school regularly, alert for the subtle or overt presence of religious matter in Title I Classes." He also noted the "administrative personnel of the public and parochial systems must work together . . . in the implementation of the program."

In a third case known as the Alabama silent prayer case or *Wallace* v. *Jaffree* (105 S.Ct. 247), the state legislature intended "to return voluntary prayer to the public schools" by means of a one-minute enforced silence in the classrooms. On June 4, 1985, the Court held that "the individual freedom of conscience protected by the First Amendment embraces the right to select any religious faith or none at all." The "government must assume a course of complete neutrality toward religion." A moment of silence which is not intended as a state-sponsored prayer ceremony, but which may be used by the child as he/she sees fit, was acceptable to the Court.

In summary, the Court ruled against aid to parochial schools by a 5 to 4 vote in the *Grand Rapids* and *New York City* cases, which is a significant change from the 7 to 2 and 6 to 3 majorities in the late 1960s and early 1970s. Moreover, Chief Justice Burger dissented in those cases and in *Wallace* v. *Jaffree* because "our duty is to determine whether the statute or practice at issue is a step toward establishing a state religion." Either he was not aware of the constitutional history and the context for the adoption of the Establishment Clause, or he was seeking to revise the Constitution by imposing his own interpretation on it.

Justice Rehnquist similarly dissented in all three cases because the Establishment Clause was "designed to stop the Federal Government from asserting a preference for one religious denomination or sect over others." He insists that "the Framers intended the Establishment Clause to prohibit the designation of any church as a 'national' one."[4] Although he asserts that "The true meaning of the Establishment Clause can only be seen in its history," his reading of history does not take account of the fact that the colonies and newly independent states revolted against nonpreferential public funding of multiple religious establishments.

Although the Court has by narrow margins in some cases continued to maintain separation of church and state, it has in others begun to move away from the original intention of the First Amendment that "Congress shall make no law respecting an establishment of religion," which Madison also referred to as a "religious establishment," to an idea set forth by Chief Justice Burger in *Lemon* v. *Kurtzman*. He said that the authors of the First Amendment:

> Commanded that there should be "no law respecting an establishment of religion." A law may be one "respecting" the forbidden objective while falling short of its total realization. A law "respecting" the prescribed result, that is, the establishment of religion, is not always easily identifiable as one violative of the Clause. A given law might not establish a state religion but nevertheless be one "respecting" that end in the sense of being a step that could lead to such establishment. . . .[5]

This was the rationale with which Burger preceded his threefold test of neutrality. Burger, in plain language, has interpreted the phrase "respecting an establishment of religion" to mean respecting a state establishment of religion, whereas the original intent of the clause grew out of Mr. Livermore's statement "that Congress shall make no laws touching religion. . . ."

In other words, the original intent that government was not empowered in any way to deal with religious matters has now been changed, according to Chief Justice Burger, so that government may aid religion so long as it doesn't seem to the Court to be a step in the direction of establishing a state religion. Devotional exercises in public elementary and secondary schools are not permitted because such sponsorship would clearly be establishment. Financial aid to religious or church schools is permitted at several points including secular textbooks, transportation, and remedial instruction in areas where there are low-income populations. Government is also permitted to provide buildings, salaries, and other aid for "secular" education in church-controlled colleges and universities where clergy teach compulsory courses in theology. Government aid is permitted for church hospitals.

Much aid is permitted to church agencies without public knowledge. *The National Catholic Reporter,* September 28, 1979, pointed out that Catholic Relief Services "had a 1978 budget of $257 million, about $170 million of which came from the U.S. government" and that Catholic Relief Services "has become dependent on Washington for survival." The same paper also said: "In 1979 CRS will accept some $500,000 in U.S. aid . . . for New York headquarters' overhead." Although there is no comparable investigative reporting by Protestant journals, it can be assumed that the government assists the religious mission of other churches that seek aid. The churches also have certain privileges that exempt them from taxes on investments, including dividends, interest, annuities, royalties, rents from real and personal property, business leases, and gains from the sale of property. In short, the federal government is heavily involved in providing financial benefits as well as huge subsidies to religion, with Court approval.

NOTES

1. The quotations are from Judge Fuld's dissent in the New York Court of Appeals in the *Zorach* case, 100 NE 2d at 477.

2. 330 U.S. 1, at 18.

3. Leo Pfeffer, *Religion, State and the Burger Court* (Buffalo: Prometheus Books, 1984), p. 124.

4. *New York Times,* June 5, 1985, "Excerpts From Opinion and Dissents in School Prayer Case."

5. 403 U.S. 602.

CHAPTER VI

The Free Exercise Clause

The Free Exercise Clause was first proposed by James Madison as the free exercise of conscience. These were his words: "nor shall the full and equal rights of conscience be in any manner, or on any pretext, abridged." Conscience was associated with the free exercise of religion because it was the conscientious objection of Quakers, Baptists, and others to the power of the established churches in the American colonies that resulted in the beginning of free exercise of religion. Neither the conscience nor the religious liberty of religious nonconformists was respected by established churches that used state power to maintain their dominance and tax support. Only by suffering persecution and pleading their cause in England and elsewhere did dissenting religious minorities win their rights.

The Virginia Declaration of Rights adopted in 1776 stated that "all men are equally entitled to the free exercise of religion according to the dictates of conscience. . . ."[1] Other colonies and states similarly associated conscience with free exercise. Rhode Island declared: "All men have an equal, natural and unalienable right to the free exercise of religion, according to the dictates of conscience."[2] A New York law of 1784 for incorporating churches said, "Nothing herein contained shall be construed . . . to abridge the rights of conscience. . . ."[3]

It is therefore not surprising that there were strong feelings that conscience did not need the protection of the federal government. Thomas Jefferson, in his notes on Virginia (1784), wrote that "our rulers can have no authority over such natural rights, only as we have submitted to them. The rights of conscience we never submitted. We could not submit."[4] As Jefferson used the word "submit" it is a combination of "yield" and "delegate." The idea that "among other essential rights, the liberty of conscience cannot be cancelled, abridged, restrained or modified by any authority of the United States"[5] was held not only by Virginia at the time the Constitution was ratified, but also by other states. This was made clear in the Ninth Amendment, "The enumeration in the Constitution of certain rights, shall not be construed to deny or disparage others retained by the people." The people are those whom the Declaration of Independence said "are endowed by their Creator with certain inalienable rights." One of those inalienable rights, on which there was practically unanimous agreement, was the right of conscience.

James Madison had a very healthy respect for conscience, probably more than any other person who served as president of the United States. In addition to proposing the free exercise of conscience, Madison proposed a conscience clause in what is now the Second Amendment. Included in his proposal was the following: "The right of the people to keep and bear arms shall not be infringed; a well armed and well regulated militia being the best security of a free country; but no person religiously scrupulous of bearing arms shall be compelled to render military service in person."[6]

Madison's proposal to include the "free exercise of conscience" in the First Amendment met with approval in the House of Representatives, but was deleted in the Senate. Since we have no record of the Senate debate, it is possible that conscience was subsumed as a part of the free exercise of religion. The House-Senate conference committee and both the House and Senate approved the present language of the First Amendment, "Congress shall make no law respecting an establishment of religion or prohibiting the free exercise thereof. . . ."

In early America the free exercise of religion did not hold the same absolute claim that the Establishment Clause held. The Maryland Constitution of 1776 had a Declaration of Rights that provided for religious liberty "unless under colour of religion any man shall disturb the good order, peace or safety of the State, or shall infringe the laws of morality, or injure others in their natural, civil or religious rights. . . ."[7] The Georgia Constitution in 1777 provided for the free exercise of religion "provided it not be repugnant to the peace and safety of the state."[8] The New York Constitution of 1777 similarly guaranteed the free exercise of religion provided that any action coming from such exercise of beliefs did not threaten the public safety or infringe upon the rights of others.[9]

The Establishment Clause and the Free Exercise Clause are not separate ideas or entities. They arose from the same problem of a union of church power with state power. They are complementary in the sense that they reinforce and support each other. It is the Establishment Clause that safeguards the free exercise of rights by religious minorities as well as the rights of nonbelievers. It does this by prohibiting large or mainstream religious bodies from being given government support, sponsorship, or preferment.

When the government aids the religious mission of large religious bodies by subsidizing their schools, hospitals, colleges, public charities, or other activities that are used to inculcate church doctrines, win converts, or establish a foothold in a new community, it taxes the public at large, including religious minorities, to pay for these subsidies. Such taxation forces members of minority religious faiths as well as nonbelievers to make a contribution to the religious mission of churches they do not wish to support. The government subsidies given to large churches build their power and influence as well. These subsidies make possible a large empire of hospitals, colleges, and charitable enterprises that reach into local communities to provide a government-supported ministry.

There is little danger that religious minorities need to be restricted by the Establishment Clause because they do not command the numerical or political power to put pressure on state legislatures, the Congress, or administrative officers. In general, the Free Exercise Clause is intended to protect the beliefs and practices of individuals and minorities. With perhaps some exceptions, the large or mainstream religious groups are less likely to need the Free Exercise Clause because the government is not likely to infringe upon widely held religious customs or practices. The Establishment Clause, by the same token, is not needed to restrain individuals or minorities that are not acceptable to the bulk of the people. The Establishment Clause *is* needed to guard against the encroachments of politically influential churches and religious movements and the efforts of politicians to curry favors from religious leaders or from voters by offering financial aid or doctrinal preferment.

In interpreting the Free Exercise Clause it is essential to discuss its limitations or what it is not intended to accomplish:

(1) It is not a justification for government support, sponsorship, promotion, or preferment of religion or religious institutions. If an ecclesiastical body believes that church buildings or a professional clergy or schools are necessary for their exercise of religion, the government may not pay from the public treasury to erect the buildings or to provide the salaries or the instructional expenses of that church or religious organization. Freedom of the press does not require government erection of newspaper offices, television studios, or schools for training reporters. Freedom of speech does not require the provision of a sound truck or a radio station. Such freedoms merely require that government not place or permit others to place impediments in the way of those who want to speak, publish, or promote ideas. In other words, constitutional rights do not carry with them access to the public treasury. Neither direct subsidy of church schools nor indirect subsidy of parents or children who patronize church schools is in any way authorized by the Free Exercise Clause.

(2) The Free Exercise Clause does not authorize the state to enforce any religious claims except freedom to practice one's faith. The state has no affirmative obligation to make illegal any church's sin or to enforce the doctrines or demands of any church. All that churches or individual believers may ask is that the government does not make or enforce any law making disobedience to God compulsory and that it does not permit others to impede the exercise of anyone's religion. For example, the state has no right to enforce a church doctrine on divorce or contraceptive birth control or abortion. The

task of the state is to preserve order, which allows churches to persuade any or all to accept the church's position on morals and doctrine and to influence society on contemporary issues.

(3) The Free Exercise Clause is not an authorization to impair the rights of others. Zealous religious advocates may not surround a pedestrian or a fellow student to demand his or her attention by impeding that person's progress or kidnap another in order to preach freely the group's doctrines. Members of an Amish sect may take advantage of a statutory exemption from paying Social Security taxes; but they may not refuse to pay Social Security taxes for their employees' future security because it is contrary to their religious principles to have anything to do with the Social Security system.[10] The tax system cannot function if religious sects or other conscientious groups decide not to pay taxes for public libraries, or public schools, or parks and swimming pools because they don't use them or have religious scruples against using them. Such facilities exist to benefit the total society by helping people become literate and informed enough to vote and participate in government, or by providing recreation and, thus, promoting the general welfare.

(4) The free exercise of religion can be limited by reasonable time or place. If someone or some group insists on having a prayer meeting on a football field during "half-time" in a game, or in a public school classroom during the school day, such activity is not protected. Students may silently engage in private prayer at any time in school or may go off school property at lunch time to hold a prayer meeting or may begin a school day with prayer at a nearby church or house. The demand for a religious exercise in either a public

or private school setting is not a demand for free exercise of one's religion, but a demand to disrupt, take over, or proselytize persons who have come to the school for an educational purpose.

(5) A compelling state interest can be used to deny a particular expression of religion if it can be shown that such exercise seriously impairs the state's maintenance of public health, safety, or order. In a Nebraska case, *Quaring* v. *Jensen,* a woman refused to have her picture taken to use on her driver's license because she considered it idolatry in violation of one of the Ten Commandments.[11] This posed no serious threat to public safety, despite the state's claim, as Mrs. Quaring had been driving motor vehicles for twenty years without a traffic citation and student drivers who might be a safety hazard were not required to have their pictures on their learner permits. However, if her eyesight were impaired and if she were to refuse on religious grounds to wear glasses, that would be a threat to public safety sufficient to deny her a license.

In general, the courts weigh three factors in "determining whether a neutrally based statute violates the Free Exercise Clause. . . ." These are: "(1) the magnitude of the statute's impact upon the exercise of the religious belief, (2) the existence of a compelling state interest justifying the burden imposed upon the exercise of the religious belief, and (3) the extent to which recognition of an exemption from the statute would impede the objectives sought to be advanced by the state."[12]

Although the Supreme Court has permitted the government to usurp power not granted by the Constitution in subsidizing churches and their missions, it has followed a different course with respect to the Free Exercise Clause. In that respect it has moved from a position of not honoring conscience to one that increasingly respects conscience. The following cases, which are selective rather than inclusive, will illustrate the Court's position.

In *Minersville School District* v. *Gobitis* (310 U.S. 586; 1940) the Court rejected the claim of the Gobitis children who had refused to salute the flag as required by the state of Pennsylvania. They felt, as a matter of conscience, that they could not violate the First of the Ten Commandments. The Supreme Court upheld the Pennsylvania statute on the ground of national interest. However, in *West Virginia State Board of Education* v. *Barnette* (319 U.S. 624; 1943), the Court changed its mind in the direction of protecting the conscience of the minority. It held that "No official . . . can prescribe what shall be orthodox in politics, nationalism, religion or other matters of opinion, or force citizens to confess by word or act their faith therein."

In *Murdock* v. *Pennsylvania* (319 U.S. 105; 1943), the Court invalidated a license fee imposed by a municipality on Jehovah's Witnesses who went from door to door to propagate their faith.

In *United States* v. *Ballard* (322 U.S. 78; 1944), the "I Am" cult was charged with making false religious claims and with using the mails to defraud. The Supreme Court denied to all courts judgments about the truth or falsehood of religious beliefs. The Court said: "Heresy trials are foreign to our Constitution. Men may believe what they cannot prove. They may not be put to the proof of their religious doctrines or beliefs. . . . Man's relation to his God was made no concern of the state" except when his beliefs result in disobedience to "laws of society designed to secure its peace and prosperity and the morals of its people."

It took the Supreme Court even longer to validate conscience against participation in the armed forces. Rosika Schwimmer, a Hungarian pacifist, was denied citizenship, even though she was too old to bear arms, because she refused to swear she would defend the U.S. by armed force (229 U.S. 644; 1929).

In *United States* v. *MacIntosh* (283 U.S. 605; 1931), a professor at Yale Divinity School sought citizenship. Although not a pacifist, he could not agree to defend the U.S. in any future war if his conscience told him that the war in question was morally unjustified. The Court held that "unqualified allegiance to the nation and submission and obedience to the laws of the land . . . are not inconsistent with the will of God."

The Court reversed its position in 1946 in *Girouard* v. *United States* (328 U.S. 61). James Girouard, a Canadian Seventh Day Adventist who on religious grounds would not bear arms but would serve as a noncombatant, sought U.S. citizenship. Justice Douglas, speaking for the Court, said: "The struggle for religious liberty has through the centuries been an effort to accommodate the demands of the state to the conscience of the individual. The victories for freedom of thought recorded in our Bill of Rights recognize that in the domain of conscience there is a moral power higher than the state."

In 1965, a conscientious objector named Seeger, who claimed he was an agnostic, alleged that the draft law, which permitted objection for those who believe in a "Supreme Being," in effect discriminated against nontheistic faiths. The Supreme Court concluded that

Congress in using the expression "Supreme Being" rather than the designation "God," was merely clarifying the meaning of religious training and belief so as to embrace all religious training and belief and to exclude essentially political, sociological or philosophical views. We believe that under this construction, the test of belief in a relation to a "Supreme Being" is whether a given belief that is sincere and meaningful occupies a place in the life of its possessor parallel to that filled by the orthodox belief in God of one who clearly qualifies for the exemption (380 U.S. 163, at 166).

This decision, in effect, asserted that Congress could not aid theistic over nontheistic religion, but it did not deal with the purely secular or religious nonbelievers.

In 1970, in the case of *Welsh* v. *United States* (398 U.S. 333; 1970), the Supreme Court said that a draftee, rather than allege religious convictions as previously required, may obtain an exemption based solely on moral or ethical objections to participation in any war at any time. *Welsh* held that any sincere moral or ethical belief that imposes a conscientious duty not to participate in war occupies in its possessor "A place parallel to that filled by God" in the life of a religious person and, since "his beliefs function as a religion in his life, such an individual is as much entitled to a religious conscientious objector exemption under 6 (j) as is someone who derives his conscientious opposition to war from traditional religious convictions."

Justice John M. Harlan, in a separate concurring opinion, held that an exemption on religious grounds was a benefit to religion and, therefore, violated the First Amendment's Establishment Clause. Congress could not draw the line between theistic and nontheistic religious beliefs on the one hand and secular beliefs on the other.

The *Welsh* case is significant because it seemed to return to James Madison's view of "the free exercise of conscience," implying that conscience is the essence of morality and religion. The Court distinguished between "those whose beliefs are not deeply held and those whose objection to war does not rest at all upon moral, ethical or religious principle but instead rests solely upon considerations of policy, pragmatism, or expediency."

In *Sherbert* v. *Verner* (374 U.S. 398; 1963), a Seventh Day Adventist refused to work on her Sabbath and was dismissed from a job that required work on Saturday. The Supreme Court held that South Carolina's refusal to permit her to qualify for unemployment compensation violated the Free Exercise Clause. South Carolina was apparently unable to demonstrate that yielding to an individual's religious conscience would pose a serious threat to the financial integrity of the unemployment compensation fund or otherwise damage state interests.

In *Wisconsin* v. *Yoder* (406 U.S. 205; 1972), Amish parents refused to let their children attend school beyond the eighth grade and were threatened with penalties for violating Wisconsin's compulsory attendance laws. The Supreme Court held that the Free Exercise Clause required that the Amish be exempt from the compulsory attendance laws after the eighth grade because legitimate state interests served by those laws were not materially threatened by the sincerely held convictions of Amish parents.

However, the Court, in the judgment of some authorities, has not provided adequate guidance to lower courts on how to judge compelling state interests. Those interests are necessarily linked to questions of social priorities and these are often subjectively decided. For example, in *Palmer* v. *Board of Education of the City of Chicago* (603 F.2d. 1271, 7th Cir.; 1979), a woman named Palmer refused to lead her kindergarten class in the pledge of allegiance to the flag and to lead or teach "patriotic" songs. She was dismissed from teaching, although she was not teaching her views to her students, and had no objection to others leading the students in patriotic exercises in her presence. She was solely concerned about her own conduct because she was forbidden by her religion to engage in such exercises.

The Federal District Court and the Circuit Court of Appeals upheld the dismissal on the ground that "some of the students may be called upon in some way to defend and protect our democratic system and Constitutional rights, including a plaintiff's religious freedom. That will demand a bit of patriotism." Professor Stephen L. Pepper of the University of Denver Law School noted that "the state had nine to eleven additional years to reach these children. . . ."[13]

The fundamental question in the free exercise case is: How basic is religious freedom? Although free exercise is not absolute if injury to others is involved, federal courts may be giving too much away in determining the compelling state interests that undermine freedom of conscience.

NOTES

1. Commager, p. 104.
2. Harrop A. Freeman, "A Remonstrance for Conscience," *University of Pennsylvania Law Review* (1958), vol. 106, p. 810.
3. Pratt, p. 101.

4. Stokes, vol. 1, p. 335.

5. Quoted by Harrop A. Freeman, *University of Pennsylvania Law Review,* vol. 106, p. 810.

6. Annals of Congress, vol. 1, p. 431-442.

7. Stokes, vol. 1, p. 865.

8. Strickland, p. 163.

9. Pratt, p. 109.

10. *Lee* v. *Washington,* 390 U.S. 33 (1968).

11. *Quaring* v. *Jensen,* 78 F.2d 1121 (1984).

12. *E.E.O.C.* v. *Pacific Press Pub. Ass'n.,* 676 F.2d 1272 (1982).

13. Stephen L. Pepper, "The Conundrum of the Free Exercise Clause—Some Reflections on Recent Cases," *Northern Kentucky Law Review,* vol. 9/265, p. 273.

CHAPTER VII

Civil Religion

The "founding fathers" of the republic definitely planned a secular state in which there would be no government support of religious institutions and no established churches. Nevertheless, there have always been those who wanted to use religion in the service of the state, just as there are those who want the state to serve a dominant religious expression of the people, such as Christianity or some segment of it.

Efforts to involve government in religious activities such as prayer in the public schools come either from the impulse toward theocracy or the impulse toward civil religion. Theocracy is a complete merger of the dominant religious faith with politics and government, with the pretense that the state is ruled by God. Civil religion, on the other hand, is the use of religion by the state to achieve the purposes of the ruling elite. It encourages the people to believe that the nation-state has a religious or God-given destiny.

The impulse toward theocracy is evident in the desire to have the United States proclaimed a Christian nation. Among some fundamentalist clergy, there is a nostalgia for the early New England Puritan movement where the religious spokesmen determined policy. The impulse toward civil religion is evident in the assumption that the nation-state is the bearer of meaning in human history and that God has given the United States a special destiny to lead the world into freedom and material well-being. The collective group of the American people are understood in a special way as God's people. The people, in turn, expect moral leadership and religious utterances from the president and other top national leaders.

The term "civil religion" comes from Rousseau's *Social Contract,* but it is an American sociologist, Robert Bellah, who presented it in systematic form as the popular religion of the American people.[1] The civil religion of the United States is a blend of references to God by the "founding fathers" and other leading public figures with the nationalist idea of Americans as God's chosen people and America as the promised land. It is embraced in the idea that, just as the Israelites left slavery in Egypt to enter a land flowing with milk and honey, so our forefathers left the tyranny of Europe to come to a land of hope filled with all that was needed for a good life. It was Thomas Jefferson in his Second Inaugural who spoke of God who "led our fathers as Israel of old, from their native land and planted them in a country flowing with all the necessaries and comforts of life."

Bellah wrote that "The Declaration of Independence and the Constitution were the sacred scriptures, and Washington the divinely appointed Moses who led his people out of the hands of tyranny."[2] Bellah thinks of the American republic as bound together by a covenant between the various peoples in the United States and God. "The God of the civil religion," wrote Bellah, is "much more related to order, law and right than to salvation and love. . . . He has . . . a special concern for America."[3]

The term "God" has various meanings. It refers at one and the same time to the Creator, the moral judge of the universe, and to a unitive symbol that, in fact, means very

little. Bellah, referring to some of John F. Kennedy's references to God, said that it is "a word which almost all Americans can accept but which means so many different things to
so many different people that it is almost an empty sign."[4] It
is a term equally acceptable to the Ku Klux Klan and black
Americans, to the American Legion with its "back to God"
movement, and to members of the peace churches.

Some of those who explain and defend civil religion
think of it as useful in the sense that it helps the United
States to stand "under higher judgment." Reinhold Niebuhr,
writing about Abraham Lincoln's religious convictions, which
are embedded in the civil religion, said that they were "superior in depth and purity to those not only of the political
leaders of his day, but of the religious leaders of the era."[5]
Bellah uses similar words in defense of civil religion, even
though he acknowledges the "moral ambiguity" in it. He calls
it a "living faith" that "has its own prophets and its own
martyrs, its own sacred events and sacred places, its own
solemn rituals and symbols. It is concerned that America be
a society as perfectly in accord with the will of God as men
can make it and a light to all the nations."[6]

Although it is possible for sociologists to describe civil
religion as a living faith, it is more plausible to identify it as
ideology. Ideology can be defined as a system of beliefs for
which objective truth or reality is claimed, but which actually
reflects the vested interests of a nation, class, or other social
group.

The ideology of American civil religion is founded on
myths. These myths are embodied in slogans such as "In God
We Trust"[7] and in the phrase in the flag salute "One nation
under God"; they are also evident in the idea that America

was from the beginning a God-given "land of liberty" where "all men are created equal," as the hymn "My country tis of thee" and the Declaration of Independence proclaim.

Americans tend to identify liberty or freedom with the United States. American wars have always been fought for freedom or to make "the world safe for democracy" even though U.S. troops have often invaded other countries for largely economic motives. President Lyndon B. Johnson used the Marines to invade the Dominican Republic after that government, in order to forestall any communist threat, adopted land reform that restricted the right of foreigners to acquire land. The U.S. failed to get an exemption for owners of sugar plantations and large cattle holdings. President Johnson cloaked the U.S. invasion with moral purpose. He said:

> Over the years of our history our forces have gone forth into many lands, but always they returned when they were no longer needed. For the purpose of America is never to take freedom, but always to return it; never to break peace but to bolster it, and never to seize land but always to save lives. One month ago, it became my duty to send our marines into the Dominican Republic, and I sent them for these same ends.[8]

One of the important doctrines of the civil religion comes from the Declaration of Independence: ". . . all men are created equal" and "they are endowed by their Creator with certain inalienable rights. . . ." This statement is not a simple statement of faith. At the time the "founding fathers" were writing about political equality, they were engaged in planning and fighting a war against the British. They could have said that they wanted to throw off the yoke of the British so the large plantation owners of the South and the merchants and landowners of the North might govern themselves without foreign rule or taxation. But, as one historian observed, "such a chilly declaration of fact would not have thrilled the masses, especially the mechanics of the towns who enjoyed no political rights under either system," that of the British or that of the new nation. It was necessary, continued Charles A. Beard, "to have something that would ring throughout the country. Hence, the grand words of the Declaration of Independence: "All men are created equal" and "governments derive their just powers from the consent of the governed."[9]

This statement of equality, like the "Four Freedoms" of Franklin Roosevelt and Woodrow Wilson's "Right of Self-Determination of Nations," was war propaganda, not to be taken too seriously. The new United States of America was a nation of unequals. "When Ezra Stiles paid his debts, freed his slaves," and accepted the presidency of Yale University, "he left what was known as a three-deck church in the town of Portsmouth. In the top gallery," wrote Arthur E. Holt, "were the slaves, in the second, the indentured white folk and the people who hadn't the privilege of citizenship, and on the main floor the citizens and church members of piety and probity."[10]

The rhetoric of "equality for all" has never been implemented. The poor are not equal to the rich, women are not treated as the equals of men, and blacks, Native Americans, and hispanics are far from experiencing equality.

A second aspect of American civil religion is the myth that Abraham Lincoln was a religious figure, primarily concerned with freeing the slaves. Bellah quotes William H. Herndon, who had been Lincoln's law partner, that Lincoln was "the noblest and loveliest character since Jesus Christ. . . . I believe that Lincoln was God's chosen one."[11] Lincoln's Emancipation Proclamation, however, was wartime strategy. It freed slaves only in the states that had seceded. Lincoln specifically did not proclaim freedom for slaves in the border states that stayed with the North. The *London Spectator* observed at the time: "The Government liberates the enemy's slaves as it would the enemy's cattle, simply to weaken them in the coming conflict. . . . The principle asserted is not that a human being cannot justly own another, but that he cannot own him unless he is loyal to the United States."[12]

The proclamation was, as intended, a stroke for Northern diplomacy, making it virtually impossible for England, which had ended slavery thirty years earlier, to intervene on the side of the South. Lincoln set forth his position in a letter to Horace Greeley: "My paramount object in this struggle is to save the Union and is not either to save or destroy slavery. . . ."[13] Lincoln had expressed a willingness to endorse as a means to prevent secession a constitutional amendment "to the effect that the Federal Government shall never interfere with the domestic institutions of the states, including that of persons held to service."[14]

A third aspect of civil religion is its intimate relation with war. It has been used ideologically to justify war, and a whole religious mythology has been woven around the Civil War and Abraham Lincoln in particular. The Battle Hymn of the Republic, which is sung in schools and churches throughout the country, sees in the marching of the Union soldiers "the glory of the coming of the Lord." There are lines in this hymn that seem to carry over into every war: "as he died to make men holy, let us die to make men free." In actuality, men go to war not to die, but to kill the enemy. Nevertheless, Bellah took this idea of sacrificial death and related it to Lincoln's Gettysburg Address. He wrote: "The Gettysburg symbolism ('those who here gave their lives that this nation might live') is Christian without having anything to do with the Christian church."[15] It takes a heavy ideological imagination to equate the Christian idea of unarmed sacrifice on a cross with the idea of soldiers dying on a battlefield while trying to kill their fellow-Americans in a civil war.

American civil religion never raised the question whether the Civil War was necessary, or could have been avoided. Horace Greeley in the *New York Tribune* wrote, after South Carolina's secession, urging that the Southern states be allowed to secede in peace, "We never hope to live in a Republic, whereof one section is pinned to the residue by bayonets." Henry Ward Beecher preached the same doctrine. But Lincoln thought otherwise, and so did some of the commercial interests. There was no sober analysis of the fact that slavery everywhere in the Western world was on the defensive. Mexico abolished it in 1827; Britain in 1833. California, New Mexico, and Kansas had voted to ban slavery. In Missouri, slavery decreased from 17.8% of the population in 1830, to 15.5% in 1840, to 12.8% in 1850, and was down to 9.8% in 1860. By 1860 slavery was nonexistent in all sections of the Union except the tobacco, cotton, and sugarcane belts.[16]

The American civil religion has no doctrine of peace, just as American nationalism and competitive capitalism have no doctrine of peace. Lincoln's statement in his Second Inaugural Address about God's will and the Civil War is well known: "Yet if God wills that it continue until all the wealth piled by the bondsman's two hundred and fifty years of unrequited toil shall be sunk and until every drop of blood drawn with the lash shall be paid by another drawn with the sword, as was said three thousand years ago, so still it must be said: 'The judgments of the Lord are true and righteous altogether.' "

Lincoln probably believed his own rhetoric, but eighty percent of the men who fought in the Confederate Army were nonslaveowners, and all of the major generals of the South had either been nonslaveowners or, as in the case of Robert E. Lee, had emancipated their slaves before the war began, so that God was not punishing them for the blood they had drawn with the lash. In fact, General Grant and his family were slaveowners at least until the Emancipation Proclamation.

Franklin Roosevelt used civil religion as the basis for his doctrine of "unconditional surrender" in the Second World War. In his message to Congress June 6, 1942, he said:

> We are fighting, as our fathers have fought, to uphold the doctrine that all men are equal in the sight of God. Those on the other side are striving to destroy this deep belief and to create a world in their own image. . . .
>
> No compromise can end that conflict. There never can be—successful compromise between good and evil. Only total victory can reward the champions of tolerance, and decency, and freedom and faith.

Reinhold Niebuhr, the nation's leading Christian spokesman for World War II, referred to Amos's idea that Israel had been particularly chosen by God, and indicated that "various nations and classes, various social groups and races, are at various times placed in such a position that a special measure of the divine mission in history falls upon them. In that sense, God has chosen us in this fateful period of world history."

The ideological nature of civil religion is evident in its use as a support for the American power position and in the extension of American influence around the world. But it is also more directly asserted in suggestions that religion has utility only for our political goals. In proposing to Congress during the Korean War that the phrase "under God" be inserted in the Pledge of Allegiance to the flag, Senator Homer Ferguson of Michigan said: "We know that America cannot be defended by guns, planes, and ships alone. Appropriations and expenditures for defense will be of value only if the God under whom we live believes that we are in the right." Seeking to reinforce his point, he continued: "We now live in a world divided by two ideologies, one of which affirms its belief in God while the other does not."[17]

Perhaps even more telling are the now famous assertions of President Eisenhower, who said: "Our government makes no sense unless it is founded in a deeply felt religious faith— *and I don't care what it is.*" Again he said: "I am the most intensely religious man I know. That doesn't mean that I adhere to any sect. A democracy cannot exist without a religious base. I believe in democracy."[18]

Civil religion is religion in the service of the state; it has also been used by presidents to gain acceptance of their political programs. Ronald Reagan made use of civil religion on March 8, 1983, to sell his nuclear war program. He chose the National Association of Evangelicals because many fundamentalists uncritically accept civil religion. In that speech he identified the United States as the symbol of goodness in the world and the Soviet Union as the symbol and "focus of evil in the modern world." He urged his audience not to "label both sides equally at fault . . . and thereby remove yourself from the struggle between right and wrong, good and evil." He said: "There is sin and evil in the world and we are enjoined by Scripture and the Lord Jesus to oppose it with all our might."

Reagan referred to his legislative program as "a renewal of the traditional values that have been the bedrock of America's goodness and greatness." He said: "America has kept alight the torch of freedom—not just for ourselves but for millions of others around the world." He also said, "Let us pray for the salvation of all those who live in totalitarian darkness, pray they will discover the joy of knowing God." He did not acknowledge the millions of Christians, Jews, and Muslims in the Soviet Union or the millions of Christians in Eastern Europe, China, and Cuba. Then linking his nuclear weapons buildup with those who have yet to discover "the joy of knowing God," he said, "they must be made to understand we will never compromise our principles and standards. We will never give away our freedom. We will never abandon our belief in God."

Reagan's concluding remarks were these: ". . . the source of our strength in the quest for human freedom is not material but spiritual . . . it must terrify and ultimately triumph over those who would enslave their fellow man." He did not mention his recent effort to get the Republic of Palau to turn a third of the islands' 170 square miles over to the U.S. military for 50 years. He did not mention his use of the CIA to try to overthrow the Nicaraguan government or the fact that American armed forces are in more foreign nations than are those of any totalitarian nation. There was no appeal to Americans to repent of their sin. Instead, "The glory of this land has been its capacity for transcending the moral evils of our past."

The March 12, 1983, *New York Times* reported that "his speech was well received by the evangelical delegates who interrupted often with applause and accorded the President a standing ovation."

When religion is used in the service of the state it is indistinguishable from ideology. Civil religion in America is used by presidents to justify and to camouflage immoral state action. When Christian organizations accept it without protest, it cheapens and undermines the Christian world mission.

Since civil religion has already identified American nationalism with God's will in the world, it is an easy step to assert that the U.S. is a "Christian nation." Gary Potter, who heads Catholics for Christian Political Action, made this plea in an article in the October 15, 1980, *New York Times*. He wrote: "All of us do want the nation's laws and policies to reflect the values, beliefs and principles of America's Christian majority." He added: "Why should not a nation's laws, policies and even public ceremonies reflect the values, beliefs and principles of the majority of the people? Those of such nations as Ireland and Israel do! Ours used to. They should again."

James M. Dunn, Executive Director of the Baptist Joint Committee on Religious Liberty, correctly objected to such efforts to label the U.S. as a "Christian nation." He wrote: "It is as if the United States or any nation, could be made *Christian by majority vote*. It is as if Christianity or any other spiritual allegiance could be *imposed* by force from without or above. Fortunately it doesn't work that way."

Those of our "founding fathers" who participated in the drafting of the Constitution never intended their use of religious illustrations in speeches as more than rhetoric. They knew the dangers of giving constitutional or legal sanction either to civil religion or to Christianity or to any denominational expression. They knew that religious liberty requires freedom from any identification of religion with state action. They were intent on avoiding more than 100 years of religious intolerance and persecution in American colonial history and an even longer heritage of church-state problems in Europe.

NOTES

1. Robert Bellah, *Beyond Belief* (New York: Harper and Row, 1970).
2. Ibid., p. 176.
3. Ibid., p. 175.
4. Ibid., p. 170.
5. Ibid., p. 180.
6. Ibid., p. 186.
7. The original motto on U.S. coins was "Mind Your Own Business" and not "In God We Trust."
8. Statement of June 3, 1965. Quoted in U.S. Department of State Publication 7971 (Washington, D.C., 1965), Inter-American Series No. 92.
9. Charles A. Beard, *The Economic Basis of Politics* (New York: Alfred A. Knopf, 1938), pp. 83, 84.
10. Arthur E. Holt, *Christian Roots of Democracy in America* (New York: Friendship Press, 1941), p. 73.
11. Bellah, p. 178.
12. Thomas A. Bailey, *A Diplomatic History of the American People* (New York: F. S. Crofts, 1941), p. 368.
13. Commager, pp. 417, 418.
14. William E. Barton, *The Life of Abraham Lincoln* (Indianapolis: Bobbs Merrill Co., 1925), vol. 2, p. 9.
15. Bellah, p. 178.
16. C. H. Hamlin, *The War Myth in U.S. History* (New York:

Vanguard Press, 1927), pp. 54, 55.

17. Congressional Record, May 1, 1954, p. 5999.

18. Quoted by Peter Berger, *The Noise of Solemn Assemblies* (Garden City, N.Y.: Doubleday, 1961), p. 63.

CHAPTER VIII

Secular Humanism

A major attack on "separation of church and state" has been launched by religious leaders who have accused the public schools of teaching the religion of "secular humanism."

The term "secular humanism" is being used by the religious right wing as a slogan to attack the public schools. That slogan is a two-edged sword designed to persuade born-again Christians to send their children to parochial or Christian day schools and also to persuade Congress to authorize school-sponsored prayer services in the public schools.

Right wing fundamentalist preachers did not originate the term, *secular humanism.* Long before the creation of the "Moral Majority" and other right wing Christian organizations some advocates of aid to parochial schools accused the public schools of teaching the religion of secular humanism. They argued that if the government could subsidize the teaching of secular humanism in the public schools, it could subsidize private schools where other forms of faith were central.

The phrase "secular humanism" was also used by Justice Hugo Black in the 1961 case of *Torcaso* v. *Watkins.* Roy Torcaso, a resident of Maryland who had been appointed by

Reprinted, with permission, from the July-August 1983 *Report from the Capital,* a publication of the Baptist Joint Committee on Public Affairs, Washington, D.C.

the governor as a notary public, was refused a commission because he would not swear or affirm that he believed in the existence of God. He brought suit, claiming that Maryland had violated the First Amendment by preferring theistic religions over those that are nontheistic. Justice Black, in the Supreme Court's vindication of Torcaso, included secular humanism along with Buddhism and Ethical Culture as one of a number of religions in the United States "which do not teach what would generally be considered a belief in the existence of God."[1]

The mere fact that a Supreme Court decision called secular humanism a religion does not mean that it is being taught in the public schools. The schools are neutral with respect to religion. It is a fallacy in logic to say that secular humanism (or Buddhism) does not include belief in God; the schools do not teach belief in God; therefore, the schools teach secular humanism (or Buddhism).

Since the phrase *secular humanism* has become a slogan without precise definition, it is essential that we define it.

Humanism can be defined as putting human values ahead of material and institutional values. It can also be defined as making humans the measure and center of everything instead of God.

The word *secular* has at least four meanings.

The original meaning or usage referred to *this world* or *this age*. The word secular comes from the Latin word "saeculum," which means *age,* but has also been translated as *world.* It had a particular meaning to the early church, which saw the political authority or the social system as a pagan one that God had ordained for this age. The church was the community of those who had already entered into the age to come.

The second meaning is identical with the word *neutral.* A secular school is neutral with respect to religion. It takes no position for or against the various religious expressions such as Jewish, Protestant, Roman Catholic, or nonreligious positions such as atheism. Those who subscribe to such neutrality believe that moral or ethical values can be taught without reference to religious or sectarian doctrines.

Many years ago the National Education Association released a report that included the following statement:

> In a classroom which emphasizes values, respect will be shown for the ideas of individual students. A junior high school boy began his response to his teacher's question with "I think"— and was interrupted by, "I don't care what you think. I want to know what the book says." By contrast, another boy in another classroom "thought" it was good practice to put people in jail for not paying their debts. Although this opinion met strong opposition from his teacher and classmates, he was given a courteous hearing.

The absence of a formal expression of religion signifies verbal neutrality. But a teacher's attitude of respect for persons, and teaching which values cooperation and caring, demonstrates religious values.

A third meaning of the word *secular* was given some years ago by V. T. Thayer, who defined it as a secular method of thinking. By this Thayer meant: (1) an avoidance of dogmatism and indoctrination and a rejection of all attempts by "pressure groups and parochial-minded people to use the schools as instruments for imposing their partisan . . . convictions" on students; (2) endorsement of Horace Mann's statement that the function of education is not so much "to inculcate opinions and beliefs as to impart the means of their correct formation"; (3) respect for the conviction of others, ". . . the absolutes which a man cherishes for himself . . . are to be viewed as relative when applied to his neighbor"; and (4) an assumption that the school does not supply all the ingredients for a full life. Many things must be left to the home and the church as well as to other community agencies.[2]

A fourth meaning of the word *secular* is freedom from ecclesiastical control. Such freedom is the result of a process known as secularization. Secularization is an ongoing historical process which has had five good results.

(1) Jesus is understood by millions of his followers as primarily responsible for the idea of secularization. He set people free from the control of the Jewish theocratic state and all other powers, such as the ancient Jewish law. "Man was not made for the sabbath," Jesus said. "The Sabbath was made for man." Jesus refused to identify the Kingdom of God with the political freedom of Israel or with any state or law. He was opposed to any discrimination against human beings on religious, national, sexual, or racial grounds. He also rejected the idea of religion as dominance or control by defining his own mission as one of servanthood.

(2) Both Judaism and Christianity contributed to the secularization of the ancient world. The concept of monotheism and doctrine of creation, with humans being given responsibility for the earth as God's stewards, destroyed the belief that events on earth were dictated by the stars or by a pantheon of gods such as Jupiter and Venus. Because they robbed the Greeks and Romans of their gods, the early Christians were called atheists. In turn, this view of a world created by a dependable and omniscient God, whose laws

could be discovered, led to the development of modern science.

(3) The development of modern science has given us a world view that has destroyed the three-dimensional view of heaven above, earth below, and hell beneath the earth. It has also released us from the cosmic forces that at one time were believed to rule or direct the world. In turn, this means that we cannot blame our human condition on God or a devil. It is humans that have created the war system and racial segregation. It is humans who can eradicate cholera, black lung, syphilis, and cancer.

(4) When the church moved from Jesus' idea of a suffering and servant group in the pre-Constantinian era to a powerful church in the centuries following Constantine, the church identified itself with the imperial structure of the Roman Empire and the contemporary culture, and sought to dominate it.

The so-called Christian era is marked by an alliance between church and state. This does not refer to contemporary government subsidies to church hospitals, schools, and colleges or other religious programs, which mark the church as another social institution competing for government funds. Rather, the alliance between church and state in the Constantinian sense meant that the church participated in the formal direction of society, sanctifying and blessing economic, political, and military structures so long as those structures verbally acknowledged the Christian tradition and gave the church a position of special recognition.

Secularization is the process by which society has moved away from control by the church so that science, education, art, and politics were freed from conformity to theological dogma and ecclesiastical hierarchies. The contributions of Copernicus, Galileo, and Darwin were attacked by church leaders. The secular spirit is evident in the fact that scientific knowledge and education in general are today tested by reason, by experiment and experience rather than by religious orthodoxy. Secularization is a historical process to which many movements have contributed, including the Protestant Reformation, which sundered a united or monolithic church; the industrial revolution, which urbanized and organized people around another set of values; Marxism, which exposed the church as a class and power structure; as well as the two world wars and the cold war, which showed the church as the handmaiden of nationalism and Western culture.

(5) For many American Protestants the acceptance of the process of secularization and of the secular public school was symbolized by the Supreme Court decision on Bible reading and prayer. They saw for the first time three things:

(a) the forcing of prayer on a captive audience of school children by state-sponsored worship services was coercive and, hence, damaged genuine faith.

(b) such prayer tended to be a lowest common denominator type of prayer so as to make it inoffensive to various religious groups and, thus, further watered down their faith.

(c) children whose parents objected to such prayer were put in a position of tension, of obeying teacher or parent, and of running the risk of ostracism by classmates if they did not participate in the school's worship activities.

Today, this whole process of secularization is under attack by certain Protestant fundamentalists. They want to censor textbooks in the public schools, have school-sponsored prayers, and require the teaching of creationism instead of or alongside evolution. They not only do not want secular schools, but they are not content with any kind of religious school that does not conform to fundamentalism and right wing ideas. In other words, they are seeking the right to ecclesiastical interference in and dominance over the school system.

The Roman Catholic attitude toward secularization is not yet completely clear. Prior to the Second Vatican Council, the Roman Catholic church viewed the world as inert matter that needed to be shaped and formed by the church. That shaping would be done best if the church could re-establish the Holy Roman Empire in new form with the participation of Catholic or neo-Catholic nations. That idea, in turn, led to the development of Vatican-sponsored Christian Democratic parties in most of Western Europe and in some Latin American countries. The attempt to create Christian nations and political parties and to get other political, social, and economic structures of society to accept Christian designations, symbols, and verbal allegiance to Christianity is known as "Christianizing." It is distinct from evangelism, which tells the New Testament story and lets people decide whether to make a commitment to it.

The Second Vatican Council began the process of dialogue with the world rather than conquering it, though there are some forces within the church that cling to the earlier interpretation. Instead of Christianizing the world, the church is to ei. er a post-Constantinian period, a period also marking the end of the Counter-Reformation. The church is called to see the good points not only in Protestantism, but in non-Christian religions and even in humanism and communism.

By logical extension this ought to mean that the church

should not be established in the sense of ecclesiastical control over society, nor should it expect government to compel Jews, Protestants, and the nonreligious to support the mission, doctrines, or agencies of a church to which they do not belong. Dialogue presupposes a free and uncoerced exchange between equals, whereas political pressure to tax the general population for church purposes is more in the nature of conquering those outside the church.

The U.S. Catholic bishops seem to have returned to the idea of trying to conquer the world rather than to permit pluralism to exist. They have been using the abortion issue as an opportunity to impose their sexual ethics on an entire population and, hence, have abandoned dialogue with those groups that differ from them. Roman Catholic doctrine holds that any valid sexual act must be open to procreation. Therefore, any interference with procreation, such as abortion and contraceptive birth control, is morally wrong. The law is viewed as a teacher; therefore, it is essential that law conform to Roman Catholic teaching. In turn, this has led the U.S. Catholic bishops to organize in each state, congressional district, diocese, and parish a political and public relations effort to elect candidates and to amend the Constitution with language that supports the church's doctrine that a person exists at conception.

The Roman Catholic bishops are also at work politically to end separation of church and state. They are working in an informal alliance with fundamentalist Protestants not only on the abortion issue, but to get government support of private church schools. Neither the secular school nor the secular state is supported by this alliance, which ideologically supports a religiously dominated school and state.

The secular spirit is revolutionary in that it rejects sacralized power. It resists any discrimination against human beings and any attempt to make laws or political institutions sacred. The secular spirit is the spirit of dealing with every person simply as a person, and not as a member of this or that religious or nonreligious group. There is no reason for asking which children in a public school are Jews or Baptists or Catholics. In our day, the secular school means simply that the public school cannot be used by any religious group for its own interests. One cannot assert that the public schools are humanist in the sense that they put human decision making at the center of everything instead of God. The teachers are a cross section of America and by a substantial majority are members of Jewish synagogues and Christian churches. There is no evidence that they, while obeying the Constitution and avoiding sectarian teaching, are actually teaching a humanist faith to which most of them do not subscribe.

It is possible that those who use the phrase *secular humanism* are really referring to secularism. Secularism can be defined as the philosophy that religion is not relevant to life. If God or religion is not relevant to life in the United States, the churches, including the fundamentalists, are responsible because they have not persuaded their members that every decision regarding rights of minorities, rights of women, the problems of poverty, of war and peace is a decision to be made from the Biblical perspective.

There is a virtue in the secular public schools. They do not permit Protestant or Catholic clergy or anyone else to teach religion to school children under government sponsorship. Most parents who worship God do not want clergy of another faith to interpret God theologically, liturgically, or ethically to their children. There is a virtue also in a humanism that respects the convictions and religious liberty of parents and children, that seeks for everyone a liberated, humane existence.

In short, secular humanism is not the equivalent of immorality or irreligion, but a value derived from our doctrine of separation of church and state.

NOTES

1. *Torcaso* v. *Watkins*, 367 U.S. 488 (1961).
2. V. T. Thayer, *The Attack upon the American Secular School* (Boston: Beacon Press, 1951), pp. 29-32.

CHAPTER IX

The Counter-Revolution Against Religious Liberty

A careful examination of the history of religious liberty in the United States reveals at least three important conclusions: (1) The founders of the American republic took a revolutionary step in establishing separation of church and state based on a completely secular state; (2) separation of church and state had the overwhelming support of church members and non-members alike; and (3) the framers of the Constitution did not foresee all the implications of the new "separation" doctrine and faced them chiefly when they became serious problems. The result over the years of the republic has been a continuing revolution of enormous benefit both to religious groups and to the republic itself. That revolution extended the idea of separation of church and state to education, to the conduct of the separate states, and to various other aspects of our culture.

Since almost every revolution in history has had its counter-revolution, it is not surprising that there are powerful vested interests among some religious groups in the United States that want to limit or nullify separation of church and state even while paying lip service to it as an idea.

Among the counter-revolutionary efforts are the following, most of which are products of the fourth quarter of the twentieth century:

(1) *Scientific Creationism.* An effort has been made by certain creationist societies to persuade state legislatures to require that public schools teach science "within the framework of Biblical creationism."[1] Evolution, which is currently taught in the schools, was not mandated by legislatures or school boards. It is taught because the scientific community in its various branches, such as biology, geology, paleontology, and astronomy, is virtually unanimous in embracing it. The reason fundamentalist groups want legislatures to declare that creationism is science is their inability to persuade the scientific community that it has anything to do with science.

Judge William R. Overton in the Federal District Court in Arkansas in 1982 stated in his opinion: "The creationists' methods do not take data, weigh it against the opposing scientific data, and thereafter reach the conclusions stated. . . . Instead they take the literal wording of the Book of Genesis and attempt to find scientific support for it."[2]

(2) *Prayer Services in the Public Schools.* Voluntary, individual, silent prayer has never been banned or discouraged in the public schools. The Supreme Court has banned state-sponsored religious services. Those who advocate prayer services in the public schools do not want voluntary prayer. They want the government to be officially involved in promoting and sponsoring prayer services so as to put pressure on children to engage in public prayer. They apparently do not care whether parents want their children to engage in public prayer or be indoctrinated with sectarian religious ideas. The object is to provide a captive classroom audience that will be exposed to the prayers of those with a religious message, which they deliver in the form of a prayer.

A professor of law at St. Louis University, Charles Blackmar, wrote me in 1981:

> The constitutional issue seems clear. The state is capturing students by the use of the compulsory attendance law, and is forcing them to listen to religious exercises. The only alternative offered is that of the conspicuous exit, which is a kind of coerced expression of nonbelief in what is being offered.

The option of a "conspicuous exit" is the basis for its advocates calling it a voluntary proposal.

Prayer is an emotional and divisive issue. The December 5, 1982, *Sunday Oklahoman* reported that two women who were church members and parents of public school children had opposed participation of their children in "voluntary" prayer services in their local junior high school and had received "death threats because of their stance on this issue." One of them was physically attacked by a school employee who was a proponent of prayer. One woman had received anonymous phone calls threatening to burn down the mobile home in which her family lived. It was subsequently burned to the ground.

The public school is not the agency to teach children to pray or to hold religious services. If parents will not teach religious values at home or send their children to churches or other institutions for their religious education, they and we ought not to permit the public school to become the religious substitute for the home and the church. There are also many parents who do not want the public school interfering with their children's faith by providing a different kind of religious emphasis or worship practice in school.

(3) *Silent Prayer in Public Schools.* When initial efforts failed to get enough votes in Congress for a constitutional amendment on prayer, federal officials urged Congress to require silent prayer at the beginning of every school day.

Gary L. Bauer, Deputy Under Secretary of the Department of Education, in a letter that appeared in the April 9, 1983, *New York Times,* attacked opponents of school prayer and recommended at least "a moment of silence as an opening ceremony for the elementary and secondary school day. . . ."

A goverment-sponsored opening ceremony that promotes religion is not acceptable. The government ought not to have the power to tell children when to pray, how to pray, or to interrupt their prayer after a cursory one minute. Gary Bauer's position, and presumably that of the U.S. Department of Education, since he did not indicate it was merely his personal position, is that "the ceremony, consisting only of silence and lasting for just one minute," is not "offensive to anyone." Government officials may prefer religion to be inoffensive, a watered-down lowest common denominator, a kind of government ritual, but that is not genuine religion. Government sponsorship secularizes religion because the government is not a "believing community" and it does not provide the context of a religious tradition or the example of a living faith.

(4) *Tuition Tax Credits.* The effort to get tuition tax credits was initiated by Roman Catholic bishops as a method of getting government aid for private parochial schools. The parents were intended to become the conduit of such aid. A spokesman for a coalition of private religious schools told the House Ways and Means Committee in 1972: "The very moment we put into the pocket of the parent $200 per child, it enables him to contribute that much more to the support of his child going to a non-public school, which, ipso facto, means that the non-public school is being helped indirectly."[3]

Father Frank H. Bredeweg of the National Catholic

Educational Association, after speaking about "lower contributions to the parish, the parish responsibility to service the increasing number of Catholic children in public schools . . . and other factors . . . bringing about higher tuition charges and a lower share of revenue from parish and diocesan subsidies" asked for tuition tax credits.[4]

During the 1977-78 congressional sessions, Senators Daniel Moynihan (D-N.Y.) and Robert Packwood (R-Oreg.) introduced a Tuition Tax Credit Bill that provided a tax credit of 50 percent of private elementary and secondary, college, and vocational tuition payments up to $500 per student. Senator Packwood agreed to sponsorship at the urging of Father Donald Shea, Director of the Republican National Committee's Ethnic/Catholic Division.[5] The bill was drafted by Shea and Packwood with the assistance of Moynihan, Father Virgil Blum, Father James Burtschaell, and Father Charles Whelan. At a meeting between Shea and representatives of the Missouri Synod Lutheran Church and the U.S. Catholic Conference, those church groups insisted on a cash refund being written into the bill so that anyone owing the IRS less than the amount of the tax credit would receive the difference in cash.[6]

One of the purposes of the bill was to reverse the Supreme Court decisions against aid to parochial schools. *The National Catholic Reporter* stated:

> The Senators at their press conference said they believe the Supreme Court will take "another look" at the doctrine that no law can aid one religion, all religions, or one religion over another. Bill supporters say privately that the hoped-for support for the bill will have its effect. The members of the court read the newspapers, one said.[7]

(5) *U.S. Catholic Conference Brief in Mueller v. Allen.*
This brief, which was mentioned in Chapters II and III, put
the U.S. Catholic bishops clearly on record as opposing the
American concept of separation of church and state on
matters having to do with aid for Roman Catholic institutions. It was a direct assault on previous Supreme Court
cases that denied aid to Roman Catholic parochial schools.
This is not an indication that Roman Catholics in general
oppose separation of church and state. In fact, there is every
indication that they do not follow the bishops' leadership in
seeking to reinterpret or destroy the "establishment" clause of
the First Amendment. The bishops, who are administratively
responsible for raising the money to pay for the various
institutions, such as parochial schools, that characterize the
mission of the church, apparently believe it is preferable to
finance such institutions by taxing all of the people than by
increasing the giving of their own members.

(6) *The Adolescent Family Life Act.* The Roman Catholic bishops have been successful in getting government funding of Catholic doctrine on contraception and abortion in
various sex education programs in Catholic hospitals and
other church facilities. The Adolescent Family Life Act
(AFLA), adopted in 1981 with the backing of the bishops, is
promoting periodic abstinence from sex as the only means of
birth control approved by the Vatican and is "discouraging
teenagers from using other methods of contraception, often
by presenting a distorted account of the safety of those
methods."[8]

"The law *requires* grant recipients to involve religious
organizations in their programs, and it encourages religious
groups to become grantees. At the same time, the AFLA pro-

hibits the distribution of funds to groups that provide any abortion-related services, including counselling and referral or that subcontract with any agency that provides such services."[9] As a result, the law effectively discriminates in favor of aid to Roman Catholic institutions and against most major religious organizations that do not accept Roman Catholic doctrine on abortion. The act itself, by providing for grants to any religious organization, is a violation of the letter and spirit of the federal Constitution. The result is that millions of dollars are available for Roman Catholic institutions.

In the *Mueller* v. *Allen amicus* brief, the Roman Catholic bishops used the device of claiming that the Establishment Clause was opposed to preferential aid to religion, but not against nonpreferential aid. In the AFLA, the bishops demonstrated their ability to draft a law that provides preferential aid to Catholic institutions.

(7) *Education Vouchers.* Education vouchers are government-funded tuition payments that Secretary of Education William J. Bennett proposed in 1985 at a meeting of the Knights of Columbus in Washington, D.C. The vouchers would be issued to parents of economically and educationally disadvantaged children (about five million in 1985) to attend parochial or other private day schools. It is not a substitute for or alternative to tuition tax credits, but an additional form of aid to religious day schools.

The Equity and Choice Bill of 1985, which was intended to implement Bennett's voucher proposal, would require public schools that receive Chapter I funds from the federal government to continue to finance special help or compensatory services to children who are "educationally deprived" or "disadvantaged." However, parochial schools and any other private schools that accept the vouchers would not be required to offer compensatory education services. The vouchers may simply be used to offset tuition.

Under this proposal, the local public education agency would be responsible for setting up an administrative bureaucracy to educate the people of the community about vouchers and to distribute them to parents who want to use them in religious day schools. The vouchers could be used in other public schools, but there is no need for a voucher system if parents want to keep their children in their neighborhood public school.

The voucher method, like tuition tax credits, is a method whereby the government would encourage parents to consider and to choose church schools for their children at the expense of public schools. State aid to public schools is based on the number of pupils in attendance. Government-sponsored shifts of students to church schools are intended to provide support for parochial schools while at the same time injuring public schools. The ultimate aim seems to be the privatization of education, but the stated aim is to permit poor and disadvantaged children to attend parochial and other nonpublic schools since their parents could not otherwise afford the tuition.

Nothing in voucher proposals or bills would prevent religious or other nonracial discrimination in the hiring of teachers and administrative officials or in the admission of students, thus indicating their sectarian purpose. Taxpayers would have no control over the schools they would be financing, as religious schools do not have locally elected school boards. Vouchers would institutionalize taxation without representation and return America to the prototype of the colonial era when everyone was taxed for the religious schools of the established churches.

Since many and probably most of the disadvantaged children are not members of churches that operate parochial schools, the voucher plan is also a vehicle for sending children into schools that proselytize them and in some cases their parents as the price of enrollment. It is, thus, a governmental method of religious discrimination in favor of churches that believe in privatization of education.

(8) *The Equal Access Act.* In 1984, Congress adopted the Equal Access Act, which allows student religious groups to operate on public secondary school premises during "non-instructional time" if the school "receives Federal financial assistance" and also "grants an offering to or opportunity for one or more noncurriculum related student groups to meet on school premises. . . ." For example, if a school offered the opportunity to organize a chess club or a religious group that wanted to hold meetings in the school actually organized a chess club, it would open the way for religious meetings in the school. Chess is normally not a part of a school curriculum. Likewise, a political club such as the Moral Majority or the Ku Klux Klan could also meet. Or, if a political club organized first, it would make possible the organization of religious meetings in the school.

After the proposed constitutional amendment authorizing prayer in the schools failed, its proponents rallied around the Equal Access idea as a way of getting religious practices into the schools. The law was intended to allow voluntary student meetings to discuss religion as well as to hold worship services during the school day so long as the school does not officially sponsor the religious activity. The school, however, may assign teachers or other employees to supervise meetings so that "nonschool persons may not direct, conduct, control or regularly attend activities of student groups." This forbids regular attendance by an outsider, but does not prohibit an adult religious staff or group from sending a different person each day or rotating personnel to participate in the student religious activity if the school wants to admit nonschool persons. Thus, Youth for Christ ministers, Fellowship of Christian Athletes' members, and other groups could attend and participate so long as no one person was in regular attendance.

In other words, student groups and outside attenders may encourage the attendance of children in junior and senior high schools (ages 11 through 18) at religious meetings where proselytization of students may also take place. Young students would almost certainly be impressed by a school athletic star or a professional football or baseball player asked by the Fellowship of Christian Athletes to attend and to witness to his faith.

The above illustrations of the counter-revolution against separation of church and state are not always the result of a joint effort. Some are promoted by Protestant fundamentalists and evangelicals; some are promoted by the Roman Catholic bishops; and some are the joint products of both groups.

The issues that unite the Roman Catholic bishops and the fundamentalist Protestant leadership are their opposition to abortion, to contraceptive birth control, and to sex education in the public schools together with their desire to get public funding for their church schools, colleges, and other church programs. The result of this congruence of interests is an informal alliance in which fundamentalist and Roman Catholic leaders are collaborating not only to achieve their mutual interests, but also publicly to assist right wing political candidates friendly to their religious beliefs.

Some writers believe that the alliance of fundamentalists, Catholic bishops, and right wing politicians is not a coincidence, but was carefully planned by the bishops and leading Catholic rightists such as William F. Buckley Jr. They cite the National Conference of Catholic Bishops' Pastoral Plan for Pro-Life Activities and its program for action in the political, legislative, educational, and ecumenical fields as the origin of the right wing Catholic drive to unite the politically unsophisticated fundamentalists behind the bishops' program.

Stephen Mumford, a population expert, has written that right wing Catholics responsive to their bishops and the Vatican volunteered to help fundamentalist leaders raise money and organize and promote the Moral Majority, Christian Voice, and the Religious Roundtable. He names leading right wing Catholic organizers and fund-raisers who work for these ultra-right fundamentalist groups.[10] Another writer, Connie Page, confirms this, saying that Catholics Paul and Judie Brown actually organized the religious fundamentalist leadership into the overall anti-abortion movement, which is the centerpiece of the hierarchy's political leadership of right wing politics. Page quotes Paul Brown, "Jerry Falwell couldn't spell abortion five years ago."[11]

Another writer traces the alliance to the leading right wing Catholic, William F. Buckley."Almost to a man their leadership can be traced back to a meeting of ninety-three conservatives at the Sharon, Connecticut, estate of William F. Buckley Jr., in September of 1960."[12]

Whatever the actual facts of the origins of this movement, it is clear that it will continue to be the driving force of the counter-revolution and will be dominated by the financial and legal strength of the Roman Catholic bishops who have everything to gain by modifying or ending the doctrine of separation of church and state. The stakes are government financing of Catholic schools and the triumph of imposing the Vatican's sexual restrictions on the American people. That triumph would lead politicians to capitulate to the bishops on almost every issue they decided was in the interest of their church, including domestic and foreign policy.

Religious groups and religious issues have increasingly played a role in politics. The *New York Times* of August 21, 1985, reported that the right wing "think tank," the Heritage Foundation, sponsored a discussion, "Why Conservatives Need Religious Issues in Order to Win." The leader of the discussion, who is legislative director for the Moral Majority, according to a foundation announcement "strongly believes that conservatives need a comprehensive plan with regard to economics, national security and issues of morality and religion in order to become a governing majority."

During these efforts by religious groups to win politically, little is said publicly in the way of direct attacks on separation of church and state. However, they support politically the first president who publicly demonstrates his rejection of separation of church and state. On August 6, 1984, the columnist Mary McGrory wrote about President Reagan:

> Catholic issues seem to consume him. . . . Reagan's motivation now seems to be his inability to tolerate the "oppression of the Church" to which the Pope has attested. . . . John

> Kennedy may be smiling somewhere at the sight of an American president wrapping himself in the arms of Holy Mother Church. . . . By contrast, Reagan is going out of his way to show that with him there is no separation of church and state. He wants it known that there is a direct line between him and the Pope, that he seeks counsel from Vatican City.

President Reagan had said in April 1982 to the National Catholic Education Association: "I am grateful for your help in shaping American policy to reflect God's will. . . ."

This is the first time in American history that there has been an all-out attack led by the Roman Catholic bishops, their fundamentalist Protestant counterparts, and the administration on separation of church and state. It remains to be seen whether the American principle of church-state separation will survive such a concerted effort. The Southern Baptists are divided and have capitulated to fundamentalist demands for some religious activity in the public schools. They have also accepted in essence the Roman Catholic bishops' political position on abortion. The major Protestant denominations have been effectively silenced by ecumenism, falsely based on fear of offending the Catholic hierarchy. In turn, this signals the bishops and the administration that there will be no effective political resistance to their position.

The chief defense of separation of church and state is, therefore, led by the American Civil Liberties Union, Jewish organizations, the National Education Association, Americans for Religious Liberty, Americans United for Separation of Church and State, the Unitarian-Universalists, the Seventh Day Adventists, and the American people who continue to support separation of church and state on most specific issues in public opinion polls.

NOTES

1. John A. Moore, "On Giving Equal Time to the Teaching of Evolution and Creation," *Biology and Medicine* (Spring 1975), vol. 18, no. 3.

2. *McLean* v. *Arkansas Board of Education,* 529 F. Supp. 1255 (1982).

3. *Hearings on H.R. 16141,* House Ways and Means Committee, September 7, 1972, Part 3, p. 81.

4. Ibid., p. 67.

5. *National Catholic Reporter,* October 7, 1977, p. 17, and July 29, 1977, p. 2.

6. Ibid.

7. Ibid.

8. Patricia Donovan, "The Adolescent Family Life Act and the Promotion of Religious Doctrine," *Family Planning Perspectives* (September/October 1984), vol. 16, no. 5, p. 222.

9. Ibid.

10. Stephen D. Mumford, *American Democracy and the Vatican: Population Growth and National Security* (Amherst, New York: Humanist Press, 1984), Chapter 11.

11. Connie Page, *The Right to Lifers* (New York: Summit Books, 1983), p. 168.

12. P. D. Young, "Richard A. Viguerie: The New Right's Power Broker," *Penthouse* (December 1982), p. 146.

Index

Index of Cases

About the Author

John Swomley is a member of the national board of the American Civil Liberties Union and chairperson of its Church-State Committee. He is the author of many books, including *Religion, the State and the Schools* and *The Politics of Liberation.*